Indigenous Women and Street Gangs

Indigenous Women and Street Gangs

Survivance Narratives

Amber,

Bev,

Chantel,

Jazmyne,

Faith,

Jorgina &

Robert Henry

 UNIVERSITY *of* ALBERTA PRESS

Published by

University of Alberta Press
1–16 Rutherford Library South
11204 89 Avenue NW
Edmonton, Alberta, Canada T6G 2J4
Amiskwacîwâskahican | Treaty 6 | Métis Territory
uap.ualberta.ca

Library and Archives Canada Cataloguing in Publication

Title: Indigenous women and street gangs : survivance
    narratives / Amber, Bev, Chantel, Jazmyne, Faith, Jorgina
    & Robert Henry.
Names: Amber (Author of Indigenous women and street
    gangs), author. | Bev (Author of Indigenous women and
    street gangs), author. | Chantel, author. | Jazmyne, author.
    | Faith (Author of Indigenous women and street gangs),
    author. | Jorgina, author. | Henry, Robert, 1980– author.
Description: Includes bibliographical references.
Identifiers: Canadiana (print) 20210221186 |
    Canadiana (ebook) 20210221283 |
    ISBN 9781772125498 (softcover) |
    ISBN 9781772125849 (EPUB) |
    ISBN 9781772125856 (PDF)
Subjects: LCSH: Female gang members—Prairie Provinces—
    Social conditions. | LCSH: Female gang members—Prairie
    Provinces—Social conditions—Pictorial works. | LCSH:
    Indigenous women—Prairie Provinces—Social conditions.
    | LCSH: Indigenous women—Prairie Provinces—Social
    conditions—Pictorial works. | LCSH: Female gang
    members—Prairie Provinces—Biography. | LCSH:
    Indigenous women—Prairie Provinces—Biography.
    | LCSH: Gangs—Prairie Provinces. | LCSH: Street
    life—Prairie Provinces. | LCSH: Street life—Prairie
    Provinces—Pictorial works. | LCGFT: Biographies.
Classification: LCC HV6439.C32 P735 2021 |
    DDC 364.106/60925209712—dc23

First edition, first printing, 2021.
First printed and bound in Canada by Friesens,
Altona, Manitoba.
Copyediting and proofreading by Joanne Muzak.

University of Alberta Press gratefully acknowledges the support
received for its publishing program from the Government of
Canada, the Canada Council for the Arts, and the Government
of Alberta through the Alberta Media Fund.

This book has been published with the help of a grant from the
Canadian Federation for the Humanities and Social Sciences,
through the Awards to Scholarly Publications Program,
using funds provided by the Social Sciences and Humanities
Research Council of Canada.

In keeping with the relational accountability approach to this
research, the co-authors researched and discussed an ethical
process for ensuring the people included in photographs in
this book granted consent for their publication. This process
involved describing the purpose of the photos to each person
photographed and securing written or verbal consent to
publish them. Anyone with questions about this process or
specific photographs can contact the authors via the publisher.

This book is dedicated to all of those that have fallen off the path put before them but continue to survive against all odds. It is the strength of the women before us, and those yet to come, that continues to push us to tell our stories so that you may learn from our lives.

Please read and keep an open mind in order to understand that we are not searching for or wanting sympathy, only a space for individuals to open their eyes and their hearts to spaces that most people will not truly understand until you are given the same choices.

Contents

Acknowledgements

This collection of powerful narratives would not have been done without the following supports. As authors we would like to thank all of the women who participated in sharing their stories here, as well as those that were unable to share their stories in these pages. We would like to thank the Centre for Forensic Behavioural Science and Justice Studies at the University of Saskatchewan for financial support to conduct the research.

We also need to acknowledge Alicia Clifford and her work editing the narratives in the final stages.

Finally, we would like to acknowledge all of our STR8 UP sisters, brothers, Father André, Stan, Alex, and everyone who keeps STR8 UP moving forward. Without you, our stories would be different, and we thank you for your support over this project.

In the fall of 2012, I [Robert] began a project in collaboration with STR8 UP 10,000 Little Steps to Healing, a grass-roots non-profit organization that works with people who are trying to remove themselves from street gangs and the street gang lifestyle. STR8 UP's mission is to assist "individuals in mastering their own destiny in liberating them-selves from gangs and criminal street lifestyles. STR8 UP works in the core community in Saskatoon [Saskatchewan, Canada] with ex-gang members their families, to help support individuals as they embark on a healthier path."[1] The project was with male members of STR8 UP, and was intended to examine the role masculinity plays within Indigenous street gang involvement through the use of photovoice research methods.[2] As I was working with the participants, a few women who were also involved with STR8 UP approached me to ask why the focus is always on male gang members, and why women are continuously ignored or treated as an afterthought. As one woman stated, "We put in the work, too."

I could not deny what the women were saying. When we look at any research, policy, or even discussion around street gangs, it's clear that the focus is on male experiences and perspectives.[3] Most depictions of women involved in gangs position them as victims, with minimal roles: women transport illicit goods (e.g., drugs, guns, stolen goods), are sexual objects that are controlled by male gang members, or work as helpers to look after children and "trap houses."[4] Outside of work by Nahanni Fontaine in Winnipeg, Manitoba,[5] there is a lack of research with Indigenous women who are or have been engaged in street gangs, specifi-cally research that centres the life history of women.[6] Rather, studies continue to focus on frontline workers who work with Indigenous women engaged in street gangs and street lifestyles.[7] Such approaches help us gain a broad understanding of political spaces, but continue to privilege second-hand perspectives on Indigenous women's experiences in and out of street gangs.

I do not want to perpetuate or support a Western socio-anthropological gaze, where the women are constructed as helpless victims, which reinforces what Simon Hallsworth and Tara Young call "gang talk."[8] Gang talk, for Hallsworth and Young, "runs the risk of misrepresenting what it claims to represent, the reality of violent street worlds."[9] Similarly, Victor Rios argues that such approaches continue to support the idea that researchers enter marginalized communities, are welcomed by "those who live there," and then come out to talk about their historic experience to "civilized society."[10] As a result of positivistic gang research, the term *gang*, and more specifically *street gang*, has been politicized to conjure images and behaviours of criminality, which ignores how street gangs are a microcosm of the street lifestyle, and the fact that individuals may remove themselves from the street gang but remain connected to street lifestyles. This book uses the term *street lifestyles* to acknowledge that people can move in and out of a street gang, while simultaneously continue to engage in those behaviours that are attributed to street gangs and their members. When we break down street spaces to a stratification of power and control, the street gang and their members are the top of the hierarchy, while those who still engage in street lifestyles and street economies may not be members of the street gang but continue to adhere to similar codes for power and safety.[11] The term *street lifestyles* seeks to push researchers, policymakers, and the broader community to define the specific behaviours that are attributed to street gangs, and to simultaneously reinforce the notion that entering and exiting street gangs is an ongoing process. Many of those who are deemed as at-risk to join a street gang do not have the skills, relationships, or capabilities that local street gangs are looking for. The term *street lifestyles* also looks to connect specific behaviours and economic opportunities to a local street space with specific codes of conduct, differentiating them from pro-social behaviours and legitimate means to provide for one's self. Finally, this book uses *street lifestyle* rather than *street gang* because, as a politically motivated term, the term *street gang* has become an "empty signifier"[12] that holds racial and classist undertones that support increased surveillance onto specific bodies and communities under the guise of protection.

The tendency of researchers to "speak for" is common when examining Indigenous Peoples' lifeworlds. Imperial colonialism and continued settler colonialism are founded on the idea that Indigenous people cannot speak for themselves and understand their own experiences. Furthermore, settler societies continue to understand Indigenous experiences primarily through the lens of white culture.[13] This history is important to acknowledge because it informs dominant approaches to Western research with and about Indigenous Peoples, from the initial questions to the ways in which research findings are reported back to the community, and to what happens with the knowledge after the research has been completed.[14]

To hold myself accountable to the women in this study, their knowledges and their stories, I engaged in relational accountability,[15] a process whereby researchers and participants work together in a partnership to achieve the desired research outcomes. The intention is that researchers and participants come to understand not only their roles and responsibilities within the research but also how racism, classism, and sexism impact the research process.[16]

As a white-coded Métis hetero male who has never been involved in a street gang, I have to understand how my social and cultural capital has impacted my experiences and how I interpret these women's experiences. To hold myself accountable to the women's narratives, and so as to not sensationalize their experiences and recreate or support the media-generated "gangster" image,[17] we created specific feedback loops so that the women had control of their narratives and the development of this collection. As the collection was coming together, I asked the women to review their narratives to make sure that they reflected what they wanted to share and how they wanted to share it. Once the narratives were completed, we discussed which photographs to include, in what order, and if any edits to the photographs were needed. The process took time, but it was critical to ensure the women had control, emphasizing the essence of community-based participatory action research.[18]

This partnership is a challenge to the pornification of street lifestyles—a situation in which general society continues to want more of the provocative images and narratives that have come to define street spaces, such as lawlessness and violence, creating an erotic voyeurism of wanting to look into but never become engaged with these spaces. The first time I heard the term *pornification* used in street spaces was in 2018 in Winnipeg, during a meeting with street gang members to discuss a research project to examine aspects of survivance within street spaces. At this meeting, a member of Ogijiita Pimatiswin Kinamatawin,[19] an anti-gang program located in Winnipeg, Manitoba, stood up and explained how he sees researchers coming into his community exploiting the stories and knowledges of those being interviewed. He went on to explain his continued experiences with researchers in Winnipeg's inner city as pornification, where researchers and those outside the core neighbourhoods continuously want to look but do little to support the community unless it becomes a fad to do so. The mystical spaces of the street bring people to the community simply because they want to watch something that they perceive as violent, where the pornification of street lifestyles is the continued urge to watch and observe.

The street gang is seen as the epitome of such spaces, where violence becomes eroticized to the point that we become infatuated with it: we need to see more, but we keep it at a distance. We listen and watch, hoping to see the violence safely but up close, like going to a zoo to watch wild animals from outside the cage. The women in this collection wanted to challenge this pornification through their words and photographs.

Across these narratives, we see common themes of trauma and neglect. We also see, however, that the women found ways to process their experiences, with fear, aggression, and violence giving way to a sense of pride, resistance, and resurgence of their bodies, minds, and lives. Through their voices and the photographs they share, we are invited to see the multiple roles and responsibilities that the women had within their respective street gangs, and how these roles challenge aspects of sexualized femininities and social injury.

I had asked the women to take photographs of what the street lifestyle meant to them, how they became engaged, and how they came to exit the street lifestyle. The photographs are meaningful to the women, and they helped the women talk more deeply about different points of their lives than traditional interviews. The women chosen which photos to include in the book; they chose images that they thought brought more meaning to their stories and would help the reader see what and how the women see themselves.

As noted earlier, women's involvement in street gangs is most often understood as a supporting role, where they look after the home, are used as mules to transport drugs and other illegal goods, and are involved in the sex trade, primarily through coercion.[20] Despite the narratives shared by the Indigenous women in this collection that resoundingly counter these views, research on Indigenous girls and women and street gangs continues to support a gendered approach to street violence. Specifically, Indigenous women are understood as sexual objects controlled by male gang members, which means that the dominant narratives centre on hypersexualized femininities,[21] and pay little attention to the impacts of the intersection of class, race, and gender on women's identities as sisters, partners, mothers, and even grandmothers.[22] These dominant narratives also overlook the multiple roles women hold within street gang hierarchies. As a result of Lombrosian undertones, Indigenous women are portrayed as passive victims in their involvement with street gangs, with a strong focus on social injury as the primary reason for involvement.[23] Cesare Lombroso (1835–1906), anthropological criminologist and founder of the Italian School of Positivist Criminology, researched gendered differences of crime. Lombroso suggested that women who commit acts of violence are mentally and emotionally unstable, while men commit crimes because of their aggressiveness. Lombroso's work established the idea that crime is gendered, or more specifically based on biological differences between men and women. This idea has long impacted how we understand pathways to criminological behaviours.[24]

For Jana Grekul and Petrina LaRocque, Indigenous female gang involvement is linked to social injury, where "gang-involved girls tend to come from more disadvantaged backgrounds and, once gang involved, face a number of additional, gender-based risks."[25] Social injury, in other words, refers to the ways that individuals are negatively impacted or disadvantaged by their social identity, pushing some to engage in street gangs. Social injury is important, as it allows for an intersectional approach to understanding the complex social realities that Indigenous women face in Canadian society (as well as men, which Grekul and LaRocque acknowledge). It also aids in a critical approach that asks why Indigenous women face a disproportionately greater number of risks than non-Indigenous women in Canada. However, most often, these discussions cite colonization as a historical event that causes trauma, rather than examining settler colonialism and the social structures that continue to create spaces where social injury is understood to manifest, specifically in spaces of poverty.[26]

The women's intent, whose narratives frame this work, is to challenge peoples' conceptions of Indigenous women engaged in street lifestyles. If we really want to understand these women's lives, we have to get to know them. I challenge you not to view these women through their system-generated files (Child and Family Services, probation, parole, etc.), and to set aside the many labels society continues to place on them (e.g., Indigenous, street gang member, drug addict, violent, sex worker, etc.). Instead, I invite you to listen to their own words about how they have come to engage in acts of survivance and Native presence, thus challenging the dominant perspectives of them as victims.[27] Throughout their interviews, these women continuously

emphasized that they do not want people to feel sorry for them. They are not sharing their knowledge and intimate details of their lives for us to feel sad for them, or express "white guilt." They want their narratives to *change* how we engage with Indigenous women involved in street lifestyles, so that other young Indigenous girls and women do not have to go through the same challenges and violence that these women have had to endure. Their narratives and photographs take us on journeys that many of us would never expect to experience otherwise. Their words, insights, and continued engagement in survivance help us begin to understand what it takes for these women to leave their respective street gangs, lifestyles, and personas.

So, with that, please approach these narratives with an open mind. Look closely at the photographs and reflect on what you think these women are trying to show you. But most of all, listen to their words so you can come to see these women for who they feel they are, not as statistics or storylines that reinforce the separations between us— separations that keep us from building true relationships.

All aspects of this book have been approved by the women themselves. They chose what names to use for the publication of their stories. Where appropriate, the names of places and other people have been changed to assure confidentiality. All of the stories have been approved by the women. As explained above, they had opportunities to review, edit, and add any information they wished. This continuous feed-back loop process allowed the women to maintain control over their stories and shape how readers learn from their experiences. The goal, then, is for readers to see and begin to understand how the women have survived, resisted, and resurged as they navigate their lives in and out of the street lifestyle.

Notes

1. STR8 UP, "What We Do," accessed April 15, 2021, https://www.str8-up.ca/what-we-do/. See also Kristine Scarrow, *STR8 UP and Gangs: Untold Stories* (Saskatoon: Hear My Heart Books, 2010).

2. Robert Henry, "Through an Indigenous Lens: Understanding Indigenous Masculinity and Street Gang Involvement" (PhD diss., University of Saskatchewan, 2015). Photovoice is an eman-cipatory and transformative research method. Traditionally, photovoice is used as a way to contextualize the concepts of health and well-being within marginalized populations. Participants are given cameras and asked to capture images that can be used to help articulate their thoughts about a particular social issue. The intentions of photo-voice are to engage participants through all stages of the research process (data collection, anal-ysis, and dissemination). For more information on photovoice, see Heather Castleden, Theresa Garvin, and Huu-ay-aht First Nation, "Modifying Photovoice for Community-Based Participatory Indigenous Research," *Social Science & Medicine* 66, no. 6 (2008): 1393–1405; Robert Henry and Chelsea Gabel, "It's Not Just a Picture When Lives Are at Stake: Ethical Considerations and Photovoice Methods with Indigenous Peoples Engaged in Street Lifestyles," *Journal of Educational Thought/ Revue de la pensée educative* 52, no. 3 (2019): 229–60; Claudia Mitchell, *Doing Visual Research* (Los Angeles: Sage, 2011); Caroline C. Wang, "Photovoice: A Participatory Action Research Strategy Applied to Women's Health," *Journal of Women's Health* 8, no. 2 (1999): 185–92; Caroline Wang and Mary Ann Burris, "Photovoice: Concept, Methodology, and Use for Participatory Needs Assessment," *Health Education & Behavior* 24, no. 3 (1997): 369–87.

3. Nahanni Fontaine, "Surviving Colonization: Anishinaabe Ikwe Street Gang Participation," in *Criminalizing Women: Gender and (In)Justice in Neo-Liberal Times*, 2nd ed., ed. Gillian Balfour and Elizabeth Cormack (Winnipeg: Fernwood Press, 2014), 113–29; Adrienne Freng, Taylor Davis, Kristyn McCord, and Aaron Roussell, "The New American Gang? Gangs in Indian Country," *Journal of Contemporary Criminal Justice* 28, no. 4 (2012): 446–64; Jana Grekul and Patti LaBoucane-Benson, "Aboriginal Gangs and Their (Dis)Placement: Contextualizing Recruitment, Membership, and Status," *Canadian Journal of Criminology and Criminal* Justice 50, no. 1 (2008): 59–82; Jana Grekul and Petrina LaRocque, "'Hope Is Absolute': Gang-Involved Women: Perceptions from the Frontline," *Aboriginal Policy Studies* 1, no. 2 (2011): 132–60; Robert Henry, "Social Spaces of Maleness: The Role of Street Gangs in Practicing Indigenous Masculinities," in *Indigenous Men and Masculinities: Legacies, Identities, Regeneration*, ed. Kim Anderson and Robert Alexander Innes

(Winnipeg: University of Manitoba Press, 2015), 181–96.

4. Grekul and LaRocque, "'Hope Is Absolute'"; Mark Totten, "Preventing Aboriginal Youth Gang Involvement in Canada: A Gendered Approach," *Aboriginal Policy Research Consortium International (APRCi),* no. 55 (2010): 255–79; Mark Totten and Native Women's Association of Canada, "Investigating the Linkages Between FASD, Gangs, Sexual Exploitation and Woman Abuse in the Canadian Aboriginal Population: A Preliminary Study," *First Peoples Childe & Family Review* 5, no. 2 (2010): 9–22.

5. Fontaine, "Surviving Colonization."

6. For examples of the power of life history research with Indigenous women, see Julie Cruikshank, *Life Lived Like a Story: Life Stories of Three Yukon Native Elders* (Lincoln: University of Nebraska Press, 1992); Michele Grossman, "Out of the Salon and into the Streets: Contextualizing Australian Indigenous Women's Writing," *Women's Writing* 5, no. 2 (1998): 169–92; Jyl M. Wheaton-Abraham, "Decolonization and Life History Research: The Life of a Native Woman," *IK: Other Ways of Knowing* (May 2016): 112–21.

7. See Grekul and LaRocque, "'Hope Is Absolute.'"

8. Simon Hallsworth, *The Gang and Beyond: Interpreting Violent Street Worlds* (New York: Palgrave MacMillan, 2013); Simon Hallsworth and Tara Young, "Gang Talk and Gang Talkers: A Critique," *Crime, Media, Culture* 4, no. 2 (2008): 175–95.

9. Hallsworth and Young, "Gang Talk," 177.

10. Victor Rios, *Punished: Policing the Lives of Black and Latino Boys* (New York: NYU Press, 2011), 14.

11. Elijah Anderson, *Code of the Street: Decency, Violence, and the Moral Life of the Inner City* (New York: W.W. Norton & Company, 1999); Ronald E. Hall, "Cool Pose, Black Manhood, and Juvenile Delinquency," *Journal of Human Behavior in the Social Environment* 19, no. 5 (2009): 531–39.

12. Chris Richardson and Liam Kennedy, "'Gang' as Empty Signifier in Contemporary Canadian Newspapers," *Canadian Journal of Criminology and Criminal Justice* 54, no. 4 (2012): 443–79.

13. Heather Dorries, Robert Henry, David Hugill, Tyler McCreary, and Julie Tomiak, eds., *Settler City Limits: Indigenous Resurgence and Colonial Violence in the Urban Prairie West* (Winnipeg: University of Manitoba Press, 2019); Linda Tuhiwai Smith, *Decolonizing Methodologies: Research and Indigenous Peoples*, 2nd ed. (Dunedin: University of Otago Press, 2012).

14. See Verna J. Kirkness and Ray Barnhardt, "The Four R's—Respect, Relevance, Reciprocity, Responsibility," *Journal of American Indian Education* 30, no. 3 (1991): 1–15; Margaret Kovach, *Indigenous Methodologies: Characteristics, Conversations, and Contexts* (Toronto: University of Toronto Press, 2009); Renee Pualani Louis, "'Can You Hear Us Now?' Voices from the Margins: Using Indigenous Methodologies in Geographic Research," *Geographical Research* 45, no. 2 (2007): 130–39; Shawn Wilson, *Research Is Ceremony: Indigenous Research Methods* (Winnipeg: Fernwood Press, 2008).

15. Robert Henry, Caroline Tait, and STR8 UP, "Creating Ethical Research Partnerships: Relational Accountability in Action," *Engaged Scholar Journal* 2, no. 1 (2017): 183–204; Henry and Gabel, "It's Not Just a Picture"; Wilson, *Research Is Ceremony*.

16. Willie Ermine, "The Ethical Space of Engagement," *Indigenous Law Journal,* no. 6 (2007): 193–203; Henry, Tait, and STR8 UP, "Creating Ethical Research Partnerships."

17. Hallsworth, *The Gang and Beyond*; Louis Kontos, David Brotherton, and Luis Barrios, eds., *Gangs and Society*: *Alternative Perspectives* (New York: Columbia University Press, 2005).

18. Castleden et al., "Modifying Photovoice"; Barbara A. Israel et al., "Critical Issues in Developing and Following CBPR Principles," in *Community-Based*

Participatory Research for Health: Advancing Social and Health Equities, 3rd ed., ed. Nina Wallerstein, Bonnie Duran, John G. Oetzel, and Meredith Minkler (San Francisco: John Wiley & Sons, 2018), 31–46.

19. Elizabeth Comack, Lawrence Deane, Larry Morrissette, and Jim Silver, *Indians Wear Red: Colonialism, Resistance, and Aboriginal Street Gangs* (Winnipeg: Fernwood Press, 2013).

20. Grekul and LaRocque, "'Hope Is Absolute'"; Totten and Native Women's Association of Canada, "Investigating the Linkages."

21. Grekul and LaRocque, "'Hope Is Absolute'"; Totten and Native Women's Association of Canada, "Investigating the Linkages."

22. Fontaine, "Surviving Colonization."

23. Grekul and LaRocque, "'Hope Is Absolute,'" 133.

24. For a deeper analysis of the impacts of Lombroso's work, see James W. Messerschmidt, *Flesh and Blood: Adolescent Gender Diversity and Violence* (Lanham, MD: Rowan and Littlefield, 2004).

25. Grekul and LaRocque, "'Hope Is Absolute,'" 133.

26. Robert Henry, "'I Claim in the Name of...': Indigenous Street Gangs and Politics of Recognition in Prairie Cities," in *Settler City Limits: Indigenous Resurgence and Colonial Violence in the Urban Prairie West*, ed. Heather Dorries, Robert Henry, David Hugill, Tyler McCreary, and Julie Tomiak (Winnipeg: University of Manitoba Press, 2019), 222–47.

27. Gerald Vizenor, *Surivance: Narratives of Native Presence* (Lincoln: University of Nebraska Press, 2008).

Amber

I was born here in Saskatoon and my early life was pretty chaotic.

I don't remember my biological mom when I was growing up. I was told that my dad was killed two months after I was born. I don't know if it was a pimp or drug war, but I'm pretty sure it was both because my dad was a pimp and a drug dealer. From what people say, he was a pretty good guy. Actually, it's weird 'cause I forgave his killer. I never thought my dad was a bad guy because no one told me anything bad about him. Maybe my dad abused my mom. I never thought like that about him 'cause he was always my hero. I always blamed my mom for his death even though I didn't know either of them. However, when I met his killer, I learned that my dad wasn't the greatest guy at all. So it was really a growing experience. I learned to look at things from…I learned to look at things a little bit differently from that day. Not just from my perspective, but to see it from other people's too.

When I was two months old, my dad died and my mom went to him. She left me for my dead dad. Yeah. She left me at my auntie's but she had two boys of her own. I've met my biological mom, but I don't get along with her. She knows where I am, I know where she is. She's so vain! She doesn't have a motherly bone in her body, at all...

When I was three years old, I was adopted. It was arranged by my dad's cousin that I would be adopted by a family. So I felt like I was kind of sold, and looking back on it now, I was paying off or I was working off a deal that was made. Ok, her dad got killed, her mom left her, you take her and be her parent to the best of your ability...the best way you guys can and she'll work for you forever. You know, an exchange and the abuse happened, it was horrible...

Besides me, there were seven other children in my foster home and everyone was competing for attention. It was diffi-cult because we couldn't just go up to mom and dad, you know, and get a hug from them. You couldn't jump on their lap or anything like that. We never really got attention from my mom unless we got into trouble, so that's pretty much how it became. When I was little I remember that I felt like I was always backed into a corner. From the time that I was three until we moved to the hood.

We had a two-storey house and I wasn't allowed to go upstairs, but the other kids could go wherever. I remember sneaking upstairs to peek around the corner of the staircase and I see the mother hugging her kids.

The kids were climbing on her and she would be loving them. I'd think, ok well I have to get that, that's what I need to get. This was when I was three or four.

I spent a lot of time alone in my room and would play records as I had a record player with all the records I wanted. I would make up these little dances to the songs. I would listen to them over and over until I learned them all. I learned to sing them word by word. I don't think my mom actually knew that at all. So I got lost in the music and my dancing. The idea of it was that if I could perform this dance, if I could show her that I knew all these words to the song, and if I get this done, then she'll love me. Then I'll be able to sit on her lap and get that love.

I must have gotten that idea from church as we all went to Sunday school. I remember it was such a big thing to remember the last week's verse. The teacher would give us homework and if you remembered, you got praised. So I figured, ok that's how I could get love. I have to get this task finished and she'll be proud of me. She'll like it and so the music was one way that I could do that for her. That idea went out the window after S was adopted, but I didn't notice right way.

This other girl got adopted later and we got bunk beds. They told me that she would be my sister and I thought, ok. I saw from church that sisters loved each and protected each other. They stood side by side with each other. So I clung on to S like that. This was going to be my protector and my guardian, and I was going to be the same to her. We separated our clothes and we folded her clothes a certain way and we put the records a certain way. I told her that those were my records and she understood that was something important to me, so she didn't bother to try to boss me around about it. We became close really quick, but I also felt like she was trouble. Like, I didn't want her around 'cause she stole my thunder. I thought, there goes my chance of getting that love as she was one more person to deal with.

S must have had it rough already before she came to live with us. I remember the first day she went to school. I woke up in the morning and I remember S tapping with her boot or something on the bottom stairs. It caught my ears so I crawled and peeped...like I was really good at sneaking around and being quiet already. I remember I looked down and she had what looked like a rotten apple but I know it was something special to her.

She showed me this piece of food and the little vent where she pulled it out from. Then she pointed to me like you can have it and right then I thought this is something I can eat later. I remember from then on life became about these little missions between us and our stepmom.

Things went from calm to hectic in the house soon after. I was getting used to more people and it was just chaotic. Soon after S came, my stepmom got gallstones. There were six kids now in the house, with the girls upstairs in a room and the boys downstairs in a room. Man, it was just chaotic all the time. I remember the most peaceful times were when I was alone with my music and teaching myself to read. I don't think my stepmom knew that. Our dog, Lady, had puppies and I remember watching her mothering the puppies and thinking, ok that's love. But I didn't know that I could have it or that I was worthy of it. I figured 'cause the person who I was supposed to call mom didn't do that for me. That it was just something I was to see, not something *for* me. So survival became my number one focus. I just worried about surviving.

Before I could go to school, I would wait for S after school. I'd sit on the bunk and look out the window. I would just stare in the direction of the school. I'd wait for her to come home and when she'd come home, I'd pretend to be asleep or I would pretend to be busy doing something to please her instead of pleasing my mom. I did this 'cause I thought I was second in line to her. And it just became this whole game.

When my mom had her gallstones, I remember that us kids would go stay with the pastor's wife or we would go stay with this other lady from church. I really liked staying with the one lady 'cause she would give us popcorn and… it was weird 'cause I remember when we were getting ready for bed, um… I remember that she would tickle one of the boys and she was laughing. I thought that she would come tickle me because at home, every time I made a sound, I would either get in trouble for it or I wouldn't get any positive attention. So I remember just being afraid of this woman tickling me 'cause I thought even though I wasn't at home, my mom would find out somehow and the thought of having fun and being myself was so foreign. I was never just me. You see, I felt like I was always performing for somebody or I was always protecting myself and others.

The only times that really do stick out are the really bad times. I remember there was a lot of anxiety around me being alone at the house. I don't know if that's when my adopted mom abused me…and did things to me sexually, or maybe the other kids did, or…I don't know…maybe even… I don't know. I'm not clear on who it was, but I know what happened. I remember I started to notice differences in myself compared to other people. Like I have this scar on my hand from when I got burnt when I was really little and I would go around to people and look at their hands for that mark. I wanted to see that mark on somebody. Finally, one day my oldest brother was the one who kind of understood what was going on and why I was looking at people's hands. And I remember it was the first time somebody tried to be nice to me. He explained to me that nobody else has that mark and I was special for having it.

My one brother would always cause and instigate shit, basically start trouble and me and S would always get the shit for it. By the time it was my turn to talk, my mom had already gone through six kids and then there was my version. I didn't realize it at the time but my mom would always say that I was the one lying. That I was a liar. I had no clue what that meant 'cause at the time I always told the truth just like they taught us in church and Sunday school. Tell the truth, and if you don't tell the truth, you're gonna go to hell. I thought hell can't be as bad as this, but I still didn't want to go there right.

So I remember always telling the truth until this one time when S stole a loonie and she told my mom that she gave it to somebody. I remember straight up telling my mom that S had it still, then my mom got up and smacked me, telling me that I was lying. I knew from then on no matter what, my mom would always think I was a liar. I guess it didn't really matter. By then I was already used to getting hit. I was already used to getting locked in my room. I don't remember bathing very often. When I think about it, I went through a lot.

I don't remember my stepdad ever hitting me. There were times when I would wake up and he'd be carrying me to his room. I remember one time he came and got me out of bed, scared, holding me and got me out of bed. I remember looking and saw my two sisters lying there and I just remember thinking you guys gotta wake up.

You guys have to save me. I remember I thought I saw my sister's eyes open and so I shut my eyes and pretended to sleep and I remember sneaking that whole time. I would put on my favourite song in my head and I just

sing that song over and over in my head, and whatever was happening around me wasn't real as long as I hold on to that tune or that song. That way I could get through the abuse.

But we would take the shit for seven other kids. I remember after my stepbrother was born, it got worse. I thought, ok, well, things are gonna change with the baby now. It was weird 'cause I totally felt ostracized. I knew something was different, aside from the mark on my hand and not finding it on anyone else, then my brother telling me I was different. I always had this feeling... something was really different about me and my new stepbrother confirmed it. When he was born, I remember my stepmom saying, "There's a baby coming," and I remember always watching the door 'cause that's how people came, right. That's where kids got dropped off, stayed for a bit and left, 'cause foster kids would always be coming and going. I was kind of prepared when I got a little basket of things, a dinosaur, a rubber ducky, things that little kids like. I was thinking, ok this baby is gonna love me, you know, like...I can't get love from anybody else in this house but this baby is gonna love me a lot.

When my stepmom got frustrated, I would take off and hide in a cubbyhole.

I could get in there but she couldn't. One time I heard my baby stepbrother crying and I thought this baby will love me if I save him, 'cause I thought she was gonna hurt him. I thought she would do to him what she did to me. I remember the baby was crying and I just pushed my way through the kids 'cause it was always a struggle. It was like we were always a little troop 'cause there're so many of us. So I remember I pushed my way through to the baby, he looked at me, grabbed my hair and went quiet. And I thought, yeah he loves me. I just wanted to protect him from then on. I got it in my head that this little guy was looking up to me and it was my job to raise this little guy. I would teach him things and...I'd steal his bottle if he didn't learn and...go fill it up. I was smart by then. I knew how to fill up his bottle. I knew how to keep him from crying and make him happy. I was in the room one time handing him a bottle, I turned and my stepmom saw me. It was the first time she hit me in front of him. From then on, I disliked her 'cause she tainted his view of me.

Before I was in school, I would sit by a window to watch the neighbours and their kids playing. I would see these girls playing, skipping and jumping, and think, well I could do that but I could do it better, and I would practice. I was

only ever allowed to play on the front stoop and not on the sidewalk. Slowly though, I made it down the driveway through games that I would play by myself, like jacks. It was like a reward system for myself for how good I was doing. One day these girls came skipping by saying, "Oh, it's the little red retarded n----r outside today." I looked around for whatever they were talking about and had no clue they were talking about me. They went laughing away but one girl looked sad about it. I knew that was empathy and I thought, ok, well the next day I was going to show them I don't want them to be sad for me. I didn't want them taking pity on me because I thought it was a bad thing after my stepmom got mad at someone for doing the same thing. I didn't want them to get in trouble by her and I didn't want to wreck any potential friendship that I might be able to have. Over time, that girl and I became friends. I spent a lot of time over there as they had a pool and would always have barbeques and stuff.

At the time I knew that I was different than the other girls. They were like squares. They wore short skirts, their hair was tied up in a ribbon with a perfect curl, a little bit of bangs and everything about them was perfect, you know? People wanted their attention but they were bossy. They would boss people around. Like if they wanted something, they got it.

I remember never wanting to be like my stepmom. I remember looking at her, being disgusted and hating everything she was. She was mean and controlling, but also nervous and scared. I guess she really wasn't in control at all. The one thing though that I did like about her was her leadership skills and how she could command respect when she walked into a room. That's what I wanted to know how to get. As I got older, I realized that it wasn't respect...people feared her, people were scared of her. And I started noticing she was different around people than she was around us kids.

Remember I told you about the little girls and them calling me a red n----r. I didn't get it at the time because I didn't know what it meant. But you see I was always different than my siblings, not just because I was adopted, but because of the colour of my skin. They were all light skinned. They looked white. My stepmom looked white. I remember in the summer time I would get really, really dark but to me it made no difference.

I knew nothing about race. I knew nothing about skin colour. They told me one day, "you are an Indian" and I was like, ok. It wasn't till I was seven and a half and I started school. I was called

n----r baby on the playground by the kids. I thought it was a candy, those small black candies that they used to sell. So I went and stole some from a store and thought these kids were gonna be my friend 'cause I have n----r babies. But I didn't realize I was the n----r baby. That's what started to teach me about race. That I was different than others because of the colour of my skin and hair.

Even though there were some issues that I had in school, it was great. I looked forward to school because I knew how to write and read but I had a speech impediment. I remember I always looked forward to speech therapy 'cause I got a box of juice and an orange or apple.

I don't remember having any friends. I mean, I probably did have friends but, not remembering having one friend who would play with me or anything. I had this routine at recess.

The bell would ring and, I would go outside to the tree line and look for stuff. Nothing in particular, just looking. I'd look in the dirt, under rocks, and if there was nothing, I would circle the skating rink and look. The school was where the doors and windows were. I remember one time I found a loonie. I remember thinking, ok I can hide this loonie and no one will know where it is. So I put it under a rock and the next day these boys were by the rock. They were playing marbles and I went running over. I picked up the rock to try to get the loonie and this little boy saw it. He put his hand there and I dropped the rock as his hands got there. This rock was huge, and I remember stepping back when I saw the look on the boy's face. I thought I broke his hand. After that the school sent me to the school counsellor and it was scary. This person was asking me if things were alright at home, and I knew they weren't. I remember sitting there and thinking, oh my God, I'm in trouble. I didn't say anything and of course I got a licking…It must have been bad 'cause my mom kept me out of school for couple days. When I went back I remember one of the teachers ushered me in and I flinched. She asked if she could see under my shirt and I said no you can't. I said I went sliding last night and fell off the wagon. That was the biggest lie I told. I said my stepmom treats me good and there was nothing wrong at home. I didn't stay at the school for very long and was soon sent to a boarding school.

I remember the first night there, I woke up in the middle of the night to pat my hair out of habit and it was gone. I mean half of it was gone. I was touching it when it came out in my hand. I got up and started pulling my hair out and, holy shit, was I crying. I was like, leave my hair. I was thinking about earlier, when we were doing crafts and there was this big box of scissors. I looked and I could see the scissors under my sister's bed and I thought, holy shit. So I went back to sleep. I didn't have my hat anymore and I remember feeling closed in. I didn't want to talk to anybody. I didn't want anyone to see me. I was trying to hide from everybody and there was no way to do that 'cause there was always somebody around.

I started smoking when I was twelve, using weed at fifteen, and crack at eighteen. Weed became my comfort because I was anorexic and it helped me eat and calm my nerves. Because everyone that I hung out with did it too, I thought it was normal. It was at the boarding school that I started to learn how to steal from the other girls there.

We were out one time and got caught stealing. I told everyone to give me their shit and I would take the blame. It was at school so I was sent to the counsellor because they saw it as a way of acting out. After taking the fall, I started to get respect from the older girls at the school. I started to have little sisters who would look up to me and in turn I would look out for them.

See, there it was a big thing to be clean, but we could only shower every second day because there were only four showers. We only had fifteen minutes. In that fifteen minutes you had to get your face washed, your teeth brushed, your hair combed and styled. You had to be done and in line to eat breakfast. It was just always a rush to get those things done. A lot of times I'd be eating breakfast and my hair wouldn't be done. It would just be combed out and wet. I hated it.

At the school I found that I hung out more with the boys than the girls. See, the girls always wanted to fix their hair and play...get ready for the boys, basically. And I didn't know how to fix my hair. The boys would always play sports and I loved sports...I don't know, I just felt like doing my hair, nails, and stuff was a waste of time. The boys were always out catching frogs, hunting gophers, making rafts on the creek, fishing, or doing active stuff.

But at the same time, remember I said I was anorexic, that happened when my step-parents were getting a divorce and I was living with my stepdad on the reserve. I don't know why, I just...I stopped eating. I...didn't want to eat anymore and...every time I skipped a meal...I felt a sense of pride or accomplishment. That went on for like a month and I didn't think anybody had noticed 'cause nobody said anything, right. Until one day I got called into the office.

I went into the office where there were social workers, a doctor, and the guidance counsellor. The guidance counsellor asked me if there was anything wrong and I said no. I turned around to leave the room, I got light-headed and fainted. I remember I came to and was on the couch in the office and they were all looking at me. I jumped up and said, I gotta go, my bus is leaving, because I thought it was after school. The teacher and social worker asked me if I needed anything and I said no. At the time I wouldn't eat a meal at all. I would just drink water and I did that for like almost a month. Living on next to nothing, which was stupid. I became anorexic because of what I couldn't control in my life. My diet was the only thing that I could control at this time.

I think...like growing up I knew I was a girl and I knew a girl should be pretty, wear makeup, and, you know, have a pink ponytail in your hair, be adored. I just...I never was, until boarding school. It was there where I got a lot of attention from guys, especially new guys. I would see the other girls and they would be kissing and all this stuff and I would wonder, wow how do you guys do that? To me my body was sacred and my body was already taken from me at a young age. So I tried to...I guess in a way I tried to maintain my...I just had to protect myself. I had to protect my body.

At the boarding school, they had this couples' walk, where couples would go for a walk. I was always too shy when I knew that it would be coming up and I would get really nervous. Oh my God, I didn't want to feel like...that little girl again.

My guy and I would more wrestle around. But because of our past we were physically fucked up I guess and it really confused him and I pushed him away eventually. I didn't want to have sex. I didn't want to. I think that's why, instead of letting him hold me or hold my hand or being that girlfriend, I chose to push him away 'cause I didn't want him to...I was already fucked up from my childhood as in what's it like to have sex and be committed. To me it was a bad thing. It wasn't something good for me to enjoy.

Then I started to hang out with another guy who was different 'cause he didn't care.

Even though I didn't want sex, I wanted to be seen. I wanted to be noticed. I wanted that attention from men but it was very uncomfortable at fifteen, sixteen, seventeen. I was stupid and naïve. I wasn't ready for that attention. I saw my sister go through all this... guys chasing her and her pushing them away. I didn't have a good view of that

kind of attention from them. On the one hand, I thought I'm too good for anybody, and yuck why would I want somebody to touch me, I don't want germs, right. And then there was that part of me that...I wasn't good enough for it.

The guy that I saw at the boarding school would go to Regina once in a while and he would tell me about his adventures there. How he went about pimping out girls there and other stuff, he told me everything. He told me how he kept his girls and which type of girls were easy to pimp, how you can get them addicted to something, so they want to do it for you, you know? Man, like, looking back on it, I don't know, it's kinda weird, like playing a tape while you're sleeping. You learn that tape in your sleep. I was subconsciously taking all of the stuff in.

Every time I came back to Saskatoon for the weekend or holidays from boarding school, my friends were always there waiting for me. So I would always clique up with them. At this time, I would hear them talk about these gangs and one that was just women. It was older women who sold their bodies. That was the thing to do but they did it themselves, right. No guy pimps, just the women. That's what we looked up to at the time. That's who we kind of idolized. They were mean, they were tough, they could fight...like the name Pussy Posse. That sounds so unfuckable, you know what I mean? Like something not to be fucked with. I just held these women in high standards. They seemed like queens. Like they could walk onto the street and run that street like it's their street, and I wanted to be like that. I wanted to be able to do that.

My last year of boarding school in '97 these guys came from Manitoba who were talking about pimps and gangs. They had names for these groups, and I was just like, wow this is a real thing. That's when I started to learn that there were gangs and how to climb the ladder. The respect you can get and I started to see how I fit into boarding school and that it was happening in there, right. On the rez, I got to learn about my status and where I stood in the community.

I started to realize that if I was going to get anywhere, I needed to use people, my body, my name, or a number of things to get there. But I wanted more. I had the respect and people tried to fuck with it. There were a few girls I had to fight because they came after me. Two of them succeeded until I beat them up later on. I didn't want to but...I knew I had to or I wasn't gonna claim my status. After the last fight I had, people thought I had lost my mind. From then on, it was said that I was crazy...I was psycho.

I started having this reputation as a crazy chick, don't fuck with her. I didn't notice myself doing it but I was. I was being an ugly little ghetto kid and it hurt a lot of people because I wasn't raised like that. I was comfortable being in the hood, in Regina, Saskatoon, or Winnipeg. I was comfortable walking around the hood. I was comfortable... talking to anybody and I didn't know at that age that I shouldn't talk to every-body. I didn't understand the logistics yet. I just thought that I could be every-body's friend and it's all good, right. One summer I almost got jumped by a gang because they said I was rainbow jumping. I had no clue that I was even considered to be in a gang. I had no clue that they considered me in the gang already.

I wanted to be down with the Crips, like fucking Lady Rage. I idolized Rage and that whole rap thing had a big influ-ence. Everybody was into that shit. Everybody was dressing like Easy E and it was cool for the girls to puff up their bangs. I had the high-top bangs and it's all this stupid little gangster shit. I made it look good from the start and I used that to gain my reputation, but keeping my reputation was hard.

I would find my place in any clique I was in, right. I wouldn't go from gang to gang per se. I never did that. I only talked to people that wore blue or black flags. So I only spoke to Crips and NS. I took my minutes when I was in Winnipeg with the Crips and when I moved back to Regina, that's who I hung out with until the Crips patched over to NS. So if you were wearing red, I couldn't talk to you and it sucked because some of my friends and family chose to wear red.

My brother exposed me to a lot of stuff when I was in the gang. Like I was in my first crack house, I was in a junkie house, I was…in a whore house and… those were the places that I…often went. It was weird because I gained a certain respect for the money I made on the streets selling ass, it was my money.

I didn't have a pimp and everybody knew that. Everybody understood that my money was my money and I do whatever I want with it. But I also gained a lot of respect 'cause I didn't do intravenous drugs…and if I did have drugs I could hang onto them. I would be the last one at the party with a bag of coke or weed or whatever because I would hold on to it. So I gained that kind of respect but…I was really naïve. I got a little bit of money and I'd floss and show off. I'd feel stupid the next day because I'd be broke. But you know I'd be like…I had to spend money. I had to be seen spending money, you know? I had to look good doing it.

Looking back on it, I did a lot of stupid things. I always said that I'd never be like the woman at the bar that is so drunk she can't get off her bar stool or make it outside or never puke at the bar. I remember in one month I did all of the things I said I wouldn't do. And that month changed my life. From then on, I became cold and heartless. I wanted something and by the end of the day I would get it. I made a goal for myself like other women I knew would have. I would have a goal that if they didn't make seven hundred dollars, they could come home. Sometimes I had to go and collect off the women too, which really sucked 'cause these were my aunties and sisters, you know? People that…I would hate to hurt, but here I would have to go hurt them 'cause this guy said I had to do it for me to keep my status, right. That sucked. I would do it, I hated it because I remember I'd roll up on these women and I would look like a boy…I dressed like a little boy…I would get the money. I would get the drugs. I hated it because I would think that's someone's mom, that someone's sister.

From there, I went on to selling dope and doing anything for the gang. I allowed myself to be their fucking little monkey for a long time. The tables finally turned and I gained some power. I gained some status when I married a higher-up. I could sit at home and still have everybody cater to me like a boss. I abused that power, and I shouldn't have. He went to jail and during that time I built my own reputation. It wasn't the greatest but it was good. It was good as far as being a hooker, jail wife, single mom, right. Nobody fucked with me. People paid me, people gave me money.

I didn't realize then I was disrespecting it. I didn't care who you were. If I didn't like you, I would tell you. If I didn't want you sitting near me, I would tell you. I would make you feel like shit because I really thought that was what I had to do, you know? Aside from occasionally punching someone out, I thought to keep my reputation I had to be mean to people and I was. I was really fucking mean. I was heartless and...I was ugly. I couldn't look at myself. I didn't hate myself but I hated what I was becoming. But it's hard to change.

That went on for like a year and a half. I got addicted to doing it. I wanted that power. I wanted that control over them. That's what I wanted. It wasn't about the money or anything else. It was about that control. I wanted to take back what was taken from me. And I did that through prostitution. After watching all of the girls and what was happening, I got sick of it and walked away. From then on, it was always known that I was

a hooker. I had that label on my head. I don't know how I did it, but I walked away with seven thousand dollars in my hand and all I could think about was, I want more money. Like, who's next? It was like a thirst, right. I have to be really careful even today because I can slip right back into that. The life, the money, the power, the control is so addictive. Today that's why I stay home a lot and make sure that I don't go out. If I do go out, I set rules for myself.

I lost all my kids to the system, and when I lost them I started to shoot up and drink heavily. I basically gave up on getting them back and that hurt. I still fought for them or I thought I was fighting. I would get into these programs like parenting classes. I kept my visits, I was detaching myself from being a mom because without knowing it then I wanted the street life. I was getting addicted. I was getting used to being...a person that distributes. I had all these talents. I could boost or I could, you know, sell my body or your body or play the role. I could do all these things, but I couldn't do them if my kids were around. I put the streets before my kids. I don't know why. It just scares the shit out of me to be a mom. It scared me and one day it hit me everything I did to them...they shouldn't have gone through that. They were never bothered in my care like sexually abused or anything like that. They were never hit. I never hit my kids. I think the worst was maybe they starved because I fucked up on groceries a couple of times. But we always had a place. They always had the best clothes. They just didn't have me 'cause I was too busy living the life on the streets. What concerned me more was what was happening outside. Instead of these three little humans that...I have to shape and build, right. They live with their dads now. But I never stopped fighting for them, until the court closed my files in 2013, but I still see them. I still care about them and try to protect them as best I can.

Amber 15

Human Trafficking
Awareness Forum
May 4th, 2012

Bev

I was born in Saskatoon. My mom and dad were hard-working, middle-class alcoholics. They were alcoholics at night and worked hard during the day. They separated when I was two and my stepdad came in the picture, and he and my mom are still together today. My childhood consisted of daily beatings. You know, lickings, put-downs, not being good enough, everything was my fault and I wasn't wanted. My stepdad didn't want me. My mom never once stood up for me, so I was by myself. They had my little brother together and he became the favourite, my stepdad's little boy. I was in the way all the time. I really don't have many, if any, positive memories when I was a little girl. Like none of the happy memories of playing with dolls or dressing up or anything. It was more of walking on eggshells. Learning the basic needs of survival at a young age. I was learning to make sure I didn't look at them wrong, talk back, do what they say right away. Basically, I was learning to try and read their minds, what am I supposed to be doing? My mom and dad would be drinking at night and they would be fighting and when their fight was over, I would hide under the bed from him or her so they couldn't take the anger out on me, that's...basically as a kid it was escaping. I would go to my real dad's on the weekend, but it was no better because he was a womanizer. After him and my mom broke up, he had a different woman all the time, and the women weren't happy about bringing in a stepkid or a kid that wasn't theirs, so I never felt welcomed there. So I guess I was always alone as a kid.

Even though there was a lot of drinking and felt alone, I was always around family. See, back then when there would be drinking, it was with family. It would be uncles and their close friends and aunties, and going to their houses. When I was young I lived in a neighbourhood that had a whole family setting where my neighbours were my aunties, uncles, cousins, and my grandma was there. So we were all together.

So when I was young I was around alcohol, yet, like I said my parents, were what you would call the "white" Indians. My mom is white but my dad and my stepdad are Native. But they don't compare themselves to other Natives because they work, and they don't do drugs or drink Lysol, or anything. They are better than Natives, they don't collect their treaty because they are not real Indians, you know? They called themselves "white Natives." See, 'cause back then I was told that being an Indian was one who was dirty, didn't work, was on welfare. That's what they saw it as. Natives were not respected back then and they were embarrassed to say they were Native themselves. I don't even know why they were taught that. It came from their residential school experience, because my dad and stepdad went to St. Michael's in Duck Lake. They had had their own bullies and their own reasons for it, when they came to the city. I guess they didn't want to be associated with anything "Native."

My mom was a wild child herself. She used to live in BC and left on the backseat of a guy associated to a bike gang. She hitchhiked and got dropped off in Saskatoon, finding a job at Marquis Downs and started working for my dad. She worked with the horses and ended up being with my dad. I have an older sister, she's five years older, with my mom and dad. My stepdad is actually my dad's cousin and was his helping hand. My dad was such a womanizer, cheating on my mom all the time, that my mom turned to the first guy that kind of gave her some attention, and was his cousin.

When I started school in kindergarten, I had the hand-me-down clothes from the thrift stores. I had nothing nice to wear and had the boy haircuts. So I was made fun of and I was bullied...just what do you do? You learn the negative right away at a young age. You learn to ask, how do you people please? How do you get somebody to like you?

Basically, my whole elementary years, my young school years, I put my all into school. I was a straight-A student, the teacher's pet. I would go to school and I would put it all there. I would go home do my chores as we had a routine. We were up in the morning, out the door by a certain time. Come home supper is on the table at 4:30, no later, you know what I mean? There was a routine and it didn't change at all. But the drinking and abuse continued.

When I was ten my stepdad pulled a shotgun on my mom when they were drunk and was going to shoot my mom in front of us. My brother is crying, I'm yelling, and they kind of looked at each other. I don't know if it sobered them up, but from that night, they both quit drinking. They just quit cold turkey because they realized what it was coming to. They were going to kill each other. But then they became dry drunks, which was even worse. They became angrier, so the abuse, physical, and mental became even worse on me.

I stuffed the trauma from the abuse and bullying. I couldn't talk to anybody at home about it because if I cried, or I complained, or anything I was put down. I got slapped. I got grounded. I had privileges taken away. From the beginning I was taught to suck it up and it doesn't matter. It was my fault for whatever was happening. So when it would happen, I would smile and just go on with it, thinking that I deserved it. From a young age I didn't know it was wrong, I thought it was something wrong with me.

As I got older, I felt that I was good for nothing. Being told that I was fat, had thunder thighs, like anything they could pick apart with me, they did. So I had no self-esteem, I looked at myself and all I saw was the ugliest girl, nobody liked me and I carried with me. So when I went to school, I would make no friends because they didn't like me because all this stuff was wrong with me.

When I was thirteen, I was secretly smoking and before my mom and stepdad got home from work I forgot to put my cigarette butt in the garbage or flush it down the toilet. I left it in the astray and they found it. So he came over and cuffed me upside the head and I hit the ground. I jumped back up and he hit me again. I jumped back up again, and I hit him back and that was the first time I ever fought back. My mom never ever stood up for me. They were living in a second-floor balcony at the time and he dragged me right out the balcony door and threw me off. I hit the ground and I was winded. I hit the grass crying and finally caught my breath. I tried to call my mom. She looked over the balcony, then went back in and shut the door. That was the last day I ever lived at home. That was my last memory with them. That was my whole childhood, you know, just nothing good at all. So when that happened, they wouldn't let me back in. They wouldn't answer the buzzer. They wouldn't give me any of my clothes, so I left and walked to my older sister's house. I moved in with her and started being her babysitter. She had parties all the time at her house and I got to meet a lot of people.

On my fourteenth birthday, my sister and her friends took me to the bar that they worked at, and that was when I met one of the founding members of the gang that I would later become connected to. I was completely hammered and, all of a sudden, I see this Native guy walking in. He had a braid in his hair, was a bigger puffed up guy, with a whole bunch of guys around him. For me, how my self-esteem and everything was taken away, I was drawn to him. My sister told him to come over and meet me as it was my birthday.

I became the highlight of the night and I remember him asking me questions about me. I was shy, but thinking, you know, someone is actually paying attention to me. He asked me my name, and he asked how old I was. Instead of lying I told him I was fourteen. He told me that I was young and to find him when I was eighteen. From there I was on a mission.

That was my first encounter with this group, before there was a gang label on them. At the time, they were just a bunch of brothers and really close friends. So they started coming to my sister's for parties, and then they saw that I didn't have nobody. Justin saw that, and so he took me under his wing and told me that I needed to go to school. I would get lunch money from him. He would give me ten dollars to buy lunch. He would throw me a pack of cigarettes. So I see him doing stuff, and I remember I never did drugs, as my parents were just alcoholics. When it came to any of the street life, I was never exposed to anything until him. I started seeing this glorified lifestyle. He would pull out wads of money and people would give him stuff. I just watched it from the side-lines and I wanted that. I wanted what he had, so I started to sell at high school.

See, what else was interesting was that I was the first girl to be on the foot-ball team at my high school. So I had a lot going for me. Even with everything going on in my life, school was still my number one thing. But over time my attitude started. I began to fight back more, telling people to not mess with me because of who I know. I started hanging out at the bus terminal and I started finding my own crew. This led me to try and prove that I could be this bad ass. I remember this one girl telling me you will never fit in, go back to my mommy and daddy because I didn't suffer on the street, I wasn't from the hood. But I proved her wrong.

I got into this little clique where we would do smash and grabs and stupid stuff like that. One day my mom showed up at my sister's with a social worker and removed me from my sister's house. They removed me and because I was under sixteen they put me into a group home. I don't know why they thought that would help me. Rather, it just introduced me to more people. I became so rebellious at that stage that I ran away from every group home possible. I started breaking every law I could. I just did not care after that. I ended up running away to Vancouver with a couple other girls. We stopped off in Edmonton and I remember hanging out there, trying to party and be grown up. Looking for the bad ass guys. That's who we were always on a mission for, which took us to

Vancouver. We were hanging around on Hastings, three white-looking girls hanging around, partying, smoking weed, doing acid, drinking, and trying to pretend we could handle that lifestyle. What is funny is that I believe what saved me from the streets in Vancouver was that we got arrested. There were warrants out for our arrest, we were missing, and we were underage. We were flown back to Saskatoon and that is where EGADZ [a non-profit community-based organization] stepped in and helped change my life around for a couple of years. I was slowly getting my self-esteem and I really started to believe in myself. I started going to school again for them, got a job and I did good until I was seventeen.

At seventeen I had my own family, my first husband. We ended up having two kids together and he had a good job. I completely left the street scene. It looked all good, but behind my back he would take off as he was an alcoholic. So, like my mom, I found a guy who was an alcoholic and mean to me. But all I could think of was the family. The white picket fence and that's all I ever wanted was to have that family. But he was cheating on me and other stuff behind my back.

I didn't see it at the time and I had every excuse. I gave him every excuse possible. I started working because he was always gone and was never coming home. I got a job as a waitress to make the bills meet and everything. My girl-friend that got me the job there was dating one of Justin's buddies at the time. So when I showed up to have my job interview, they were all there in the bar. Seeing him again, I got all excited and started working the night shifts. Over time, I started straying from my relationship as I was giving up on my husband, and one night I got a phone call telling me that I needed to come get him. He would always find himself in trouble where he would get beat up and left in alleys and stuff. This time I call Justin to come and help me find him. We got to the hotel and opened the room and I caught him with another woman. I just couldn't even believe it. I was heart-broken and I started crying as Justin and his guys beat him up in front of me. As soon as that happened I got a sense of power and it was overwhelming to think that they did that for me. I'm crying because that was the end of my seven-year relationship and we have two kids together. It was after that that Justin and I started to date.

Because I look white and innocent I was never looked at by the cops as the type to be doing anything wrong. So I became a mule or transporter. I had all the money, the dope, everything. I had all this trust from them. I knew what I was doing was wrong but these guys gave me this trust that nobody else had. So yeah, I started bossing people around and giving orders. I could do anything I wanted. Justin was paying for my kids, being a father figure for them. Over time, with all the partying and everything, I slowly started doing coke. I would have all this stuff at my house and think what's the big deal about it? What's all the fuss? So I started slowly doing lines. I slowly started getting more outgoing with people who were using and my sister became a really bad drug addict. She would come over and ask me to hook her up.

I have so much they won't even know it's missing. She taught me that I was wasting it by doing lines and that I needed to smoke it. So that was the first time I smoked it with her, and I was instantly hooked. I was like, holy shit, that's good, you know? I told myself as long as I don't know how to cook it I don't have an addiction. So now I'm doing this all behind Justin's back and I act sober when they show up or I act really tired. At the time my two older kids were in Regina with their dad's mom. I told her I needed a break and she took them for a while.

Over time the guys started noticing that coke was going missing. Money was going missing. I showed up at the bar and got corned in the phone booth. They told me that they were going to break my ankles if I didn't straighten up. Justin told me if I kept using and this or that he wouldn't be able to be with me. I got scared and I packed up and moved to Regina. I was binge using at the time, and while in Regina my ex-husband picked up the two older kids. He was drunk and went to a bar leaving our kids in the truck when it was minus thirty just before Christmas getting my kids apprehended. So I had to fight to get my kids back, I had to sober up. But I wasn't ready to sober up.

You see, even though I wasn't in the gang at this time, there was still so much violence. I got my face smashed with a bat one night as I was sleeping on the couch. By this time, I was into needle dope and slamming, and it was the time that residential school money started to come in. It was here that I learned how to be a cook. I got up and went to the bathroom and my face is gushing blood, I got a busted face up, what do I do? I started getting high; I didn't even want to go to the doctor. The next day I looked in the mirror I couldn't believe what I was seeing. I looked at myself. I was supposed to have a visit with my kids that day. I

called one of my supports and she picked me up and I went to detox, and that was the last day I used.

I wanted to straighten my life out again. I went to detox, then treatment, and started going to NA meetings. I got my kids back and living in my own apartment. While in NA I met a guy who asked me if I wanted to be a driver for his cousin for five hundred dollars a night. I didn't have to do anything but drive. So here I am a single mom, two kids, in recovery. Of course I want to make five hundred bucks. Absolutely, for sure, no questions asked. At this time Justin and the crew also came to Regina to get me to come back to Saskatoon. I just wasn't...I didn't want to go back to him because I found out when I was messing up he was sleeping with another woman. I found out he cheated on me and I don't like cheaters. I gave him the hardest time and my way of punishing him was ignoring him, making him chase me.

So I started driving for this Native guy who was fifteen years older than me and looked real gangster. I got all wooed over again. He wasn't good looking; it was just his persona, you know? He picked me up and I asked him where he needed to drive to and he said around the city. I just thought he needed a ride maybe out of town and back. He said no, we're delivering and he had cell phones that rang all night. You see, once I got into the car, that that adrenaline came back as soon as I felt needed or wanted.

At one point in the night, a woman came running to the car and grabbed open his door freaking out on him. He told me to drive and then he pushed her and I stepped on the gas and she was hanging on to him. She got dragged with us and when she let go she kind of hit the ground and we just kept driving. He told me that that was his wife and that he needed to have a woman like me. And here I am young and looking for somebody to love me. I thought that was the most heroic thing ever, my knight in shining armour all of a sudden.

So we started dating and I was making up to a thousand dollars a night driving him and another guy. But two weeks into our relationship we got into an argument and he was driving and he punched me, knocking me out. I remember waking up and I am in the alley and I don't even know where I am. I ran home and I hid in my place and he showed up at my house the next night. He had all these flowers, apologized, and he had money for me. So I forgave him and let him in. The next day he hit me again and he started saying sorry and that he had an anger problem and made it go back to where it was my fault. It was almost like if I looked at him

the wrong way or I wasn't counting fast enough, I wasn't doing anything.

Now that I look at it, I was stupid. But, at the time, I felt it was all my fault and I deserved everything that was happening. One night I passed through the wrong crew and he came at me with a knife and he tried to kill me. I covered my head and he stabbed me. I still have the scar on my hand. He told me that he was going to make me bleed to death. He told me if I left him he would find my kids who were living at their grandma's again. I knew I was getting back into everything again and I didn't want them to see that life. It became a cycle. He beat me, I would go to the hospital, cops show up, I run, and then end up back with the guy. I don't know what it is. It was almost like you crave that honeymoon stage. You get him so pissed off he beats the shit out of you, but then there's that remorse and he's kissing you, making you feel like a queen. He is sorry, and I need to fix him. So he was my mission, to fix him. I had to 'cause he couldn't be without me. While all of this was going on his ex-wife committed suicide. That was an ugly cycle for almost two years. Almost daily. I couldn't look at another guy. A guy looked at me, I was getting the shit kicked out of me. I always had a fat lip, black eyes, bald spots on my head from my hair getting pulled out.

I ended up leaving him for seven months, and at the time I was pregnant. I didn't want to do the life no more. He told me that he was changing and he wouldn't be angry with me no more and all the other stuff. But the abuse started right back up again. I wasn't allowed to talk to nobody. I was cut off from everybody and he was hitting me again. He beat me up so bad one time in the middle of winter and I had no socks or shoes and a lady found me unconscious and called 911. I was rushed into the hospital to stop my labour. My baby had a broken arm in my womb. Two weeks before my due date, the guy found me at my house. I have no clue how he found me, but he threw me down the stairs and broke every finger off my knuckles. They were just dislocated and were hanging there telling me I was his, there was no way I was going to get away from him and then he left. I had to walk to the hospital crying, every finger hanging.

When my baby was three months old, he showed up again said he wanted to talk and see his son. He said he was sorry. I told him that I would come down and we will go for a drive to talk. I just didn't want him around my son. So I got in his car and it was one of the stupidest things I have ever done. We went for a

drive, he started driving out of the city towards Regina. Just as we got out of the city, he punched me. I tried to get out of the car and he reached over and he hit me with a hammer. He cracked me good and started to beat me with a hammer, and that's all I remember was him hitting me. I came to in the hospital. I was told that a young guy and his girl-friend pulled off the side of the road and they saw me in the ditch. My ex left me in the ditch for dead. My jaw was dislo-cated, cheekbone was smashed. I had big gouges in my head from the hammer and was completely unconscious. It was some time after that I was walking and I saw Justin with a couple of his guys. They asked how I was doing because they all knew what was going on with me when I was away.

I guess they came to Regina to try and get me a couple of times and my mom had asked them to come to get me also, to get me away from all of the violence and abuse. At this time, I now had four kids, back in Saskatoon living my life, and trying to be the best for my kids. Justin called me a couple weeks later so we started to hang out again, but this time it was my turn to be boss. I wanted to see how far I could take it. I told him, you cheat on me or anything we are done. He made it very clear to everybody I was his woman. He brought everybody around and told them to treat me like they treat him. If I said something to them, it was like he was saying it to them. My ex, who beat me with a hammer, got off on the charges because I didn't have any memory of it and he said that I jumped out of the vehicle. So he got out of jail and came to my house and all the guys happened to be there and they chased him and that was the last I ever heard of him.

So now that I am with Justin, I have the label of being his wife and I get all of his power. At the time it was a lot smaller circle and we were tighter then. So I got the power and control again. I was able to give out minutes. You were short, a minute. Didn't show up to your shift, a minute. I implemented a taxing system. People who were found selling to pregnant women or anything got a minute or they got cut off from selling for a week, I just started making more rules.

We got raided one time and I had my five-year-old and three-month-old sons in the house with me. The doors were open and the cops wouldn't move my baby and I kept yelling at them to move my baby or cover him up or something because he was by the door and they didn't. Two weeks after that raid my son passed away from pneumonia.

It was Easter long weekend and he was sick. He wasn't breathing very good and he caught a cold. We brought him to the doctor and the doctor told us to get him to the hospital for a chest x-ray. We get to the hospital, we have a seat in the waiting room. Our son's sick and because Justin felt like they were treating us differently, he gave attitude right away. As a result, they refused to see us. They told us that we needed to leave because they didn't like his attitude. We left and I came back two hours later with my mom and they told us that it was just a virus, that it would get worse before it got better and that there was nothing they could do. They didn't do the chest x-rays that my doctor had called ahead and told them we were coming to get this done. That was Friday. Saturday morning, we go back again and were told that it was a virus and that there was nothing that they could do. I went back that night and I refused to leave, saying that they need to check my son.

So they did and his oxygen levels were extremely low and they said it must be a malfunction on the machine. The doctor that was there told me that if they listened to every mother's intuition that they wouldn't need doctors and he told us to leave. I was with Justin and some of the guys and they started making a big deal and security and the police were called. I said I didn't want to leave until my son was checked out properly, but we got escorted out. So I go to another hospital, but they refer us back to same hospital I was just escorted from. On Monday I was getting ready to go back to the hospital again because he was having more trouble breathing and he was fevered right up and he took his last breath at home in my arms, you know?

The doctors said that there was nothing they could do for him and then the police came and did a full investigation in my house thinking that I did something. It took six months and was four days before Christmas that I got his autopsy result back. He had double bacterial bronchial pneumonia. If they would have just done the x-ray, he would still be alive. So when my baby passed away, I became so angry with authority, and I became even more entrenched. I was like, fuck you, guys. At the funeral and the wake, cops were there undercover and ruining that for me. That's when we became more big time. Recruited more people, getting more violent, taking over more territory, not even caring, and...yeah, I became lost.

Soon I went to jail and got separated from everybody. I got put in the hole and wasn't allowed to be around anybody. I was thinking that I'm not that bad of a person, why is everybody treating me like this? I was labelled and put into gang intervention. You see, at the time there were only a handful of women gang members, those that acted like soldiers. I ended up going to the healing lodge. They made sure there was no other women that I could kind of attach to. I was put on the spot by myself. I had to fight my own battles and had a lot of fights and shit like that. I got out of the healing lodge and was transferred to Winnipeg. I was still with Justin during all of this and that resulted in me getting denied two paroles because I refused to leave him. I found out later that Justin had a different girlfriend and that she was going in and visiting him and that was my wake-up call. I was like, what am I doing? I am throwing everything away, for what? To be cheated on. To be made into a joke. To be fooled. I made my name in prison, and it just wasn't for me. My kids weren't with me, but Justin broke my heart. We were supposed to grow old together and sit in rocking chairs, watching our grandkids, and this and that. Then he absolutely played me for a woman that was benefitting him in the community. She was doing his runs for him. Picking up for him and doing stuff and I was supposed to sit there. In the end I got made a fool of.

When I was a year and a half into my bit, I knew I had to make some serious changes. Do I want to continue to try and live the street life and try and have that power and control over people? It wasn't me. It was never me. I was always trying to be someone I wasn't. I had to ask myself if I actually want to settle down and get my kids and live a quiet life.

I had befriended a woman in jail who was older than me and she would bring her adult kids in to visit. I would tease her and tell her that I was going to hook up with her son when I get out 'cause he seemed like a good guy. When I got out of jail we connected, her son and I, and we started having coffee together and going for lunch. He would pick me up on my lunch at work and I started hanging around and after two months we started dating.

He gets worried sometimes thinking what if we don't make enough money, are you going to try and go back? See, I didn't roll over, so I got out on good terms, I didn't piss anybody off. I have enemies, oh, definitely, there's some people who aren't happy that I am done, but I'm living a good life. So for everything that I know and I have seen and I have done and be able to sit here and not have any worries, I am very one and few, not many people can get out and not have any worries.

Throughout everything, I gave birth to six kids, one being deceased now, so I have five with me. I was in jail for three and a half years. I didn't see my kids because I didn't want them to see me in there.

For me to stay out I left everybody alone. It's really the determination for a better life. I was always chasing something that wasn't real. I was hooked to something that was never there and now I actually have it and it's no longer trying to pretend that I am someone that I am not. I am not searching anymore.

2016/04/19

2016/04/19

CANT BE STOPPED

LIFE *is not* MEASURED
by the
NUMBER *of* BREATHS **WE TAKE**
but by **the** MOMENTS
that take our BREATH **AWAY**

2016/04/19

2016/04/19

Chantel

I'll just start from the beginning.

I was a product of rape and given up for adoption to a white middle-class family. I have three younger siblings. A biological brother and sister who I don't have contact with anymore, at one point I did, but not anymore. I also have an adopted brother. I remember my first sexual experience being at the age of four. After that, I remember being out of control. I started stealing bubble gum, stuff like that, and my mom would make me take it back to the store. Violence soon followed where I would just destroy anything and everything. I had a really bad attitude from a real young age.

I remember getting whatever I wanted. Except my mom never told me she loved me until I was thirty-seven years old when I got released from prison. I bottled everything up and didn't talk to anyone about what has happened to me till I was thirty-six.

At the age of twelve, I found out that I was a product...I was born because of rape. I didn't even know where I belonged. It wasn't when

I was adopted or when I went to prison. It wasn't until I left home and hand-picked my own street family that I felt I belonged.

Now that I have worked on myself, I can look back and realize I was trying to help everybody else 'cause I didn't know how to help myself. I was trying to fix or help everyone because I didn't want to admit that something was wrong. After the sexual experience at the age of four, sex became normal. That's what happens in life, you know? I mean, drinking and drugs were intro-duced probably at the age of eleven. Through it all, I learnt never to talk. The street family sold drugs. That's the family I was involved in, that's my first gang experience.

I went to a Catholic school in Regina. I was the kid that never fit in with anybody. I had textbooks thrown at my head. I've had a desk thrown at my head by a teacher. Another time the teacher that threw the textbook at me went to grab a pen from my hand, and it went into the side of my eye. He didn't apologize. I got punished. I remember it was a red pen. If I would have been listening, then it would have never happened.

I remember feeling labelled with the other Native kids. Those kids were from dysfunctional families, and I was dysfunctional. I always hung out with all of those Native kids. I always grew up hanging out with the kids in foster care, the kids in group homes, the kids with dysfunctional backgrounds. That's where I felt like I belonged.

I remember how the white kids would pick on those kids. My first fight was probably grade three or four. I remember getting violent, throwing punches, kicking them in the head, and fighting all the time. A boy was picking on a kid, I got him to the ground, I stomped his head, and I just kept stomping and stomping. I remember my older brother pulled me off of him. It was at recess, on the playground, and it was mostly with the boys.

The kids that I hung out with, I looked up to their parents who were drinking, doing drugs, and partying. I saw them and thought I didn't have to listen to anybody because there were no rules, right. There was no structure. There was structure and all of that at home, which I didn't want. I saw this through the other families that I hung out with. I'm struc-tured and I'm watching my friends who didn't have any curfew. I just liked that they could do whatever they wanted.

But you see I also hid everything and I started to put on this mask that I was doing good. At the same time that I was fighting and the other stuff, I was taking dance lessons. I danced until I was thirteen or fourteen. I think dancing was an outlet for me to express myself because I couldn't talk. I didn't communicate; I did not communicate. My communication was screaming, yelling, throwing stuff, destroying stuff, and fighting.

I met my oldest baby daddy when I was twelve. His family became my handpicked street family. He had an older sister who was three years older, and all of her friends were the ones that I looked up to. They were the ones that were partying and drinking.

My street mom and dad met each other when she was fourteen. She was a prostitute and he was her pimp. They hooked up and that's how they met. They started having kids at fourteen. My biological mom also had me at fourteen. It's really weird 'cause, there's V who had L at fourteen, and then there is S who had me at fourteen, and I just felt like maybe this is what it's really supposed to be. So I drifted towards that, right. I guess in the big aspect of it all I was a kid who didn't know where she came from. A kid who was born out of a crime. That crime became normalized in my life by other people, and it happened to me. So where do I belong?

I just tried to find where I belong. I was seeking it out all over, you know? The white kids wanted nothing to do with me. The rich white kids wanted nothing to do with me, even though my family was the same as theirs. So I started hanging out with my baby daddy at the age of twelve. I idolized the street lifestyle, where drugs, prostitution, and partying were normalized. And I was just a kid. I got pregnant at fifteen.

When I was pregnant with my first daughter, my baby daddy stabbed me. When she was three months old, he shot me. It grazed the side of my head and went through the ceiling and I thought that was normal. I thought it was all normal, the drugs, the alcohol, the fighting, the crime. Yeah, I never forget, he downed a 26 oz., then he wanted to hold C. She was three months old. I said no, and he came to try to take her. He gave me a shot but I ducked. Instead, his fist went through the wall and got stuck. So I took off with her, and he came out with a gun. I was standing in the living room and, I...fuck, I don't know. He pulled the trigger, I heard the noise, and I felt something go by my head. That bullet hole is still in the ceiling of the house to this day. I ran for my life, and it was cold out. I hid under a car three doors down, and I thought, I got to go back, he's there, he just shot at me, but she's three months old, and he's in no condition to take care of her at all. So I went back. I got a hold of my street parents 'cause they lived two blocks away just down the street. His dad beat the shit out of him, you know? They've straightened up and live a totally different lifestyle, but he's still messed up.

I thought that this life was all normal. The drugs were normal, the alcohol was normal, the fighting was normal, the crime was normal. It was all normal. And they always told me, don't ever talk, don't ever speak, don't be a rat.

See, when I partied when I was young, it was violent. It was an endless amount of drugs and alcohol. I didn't enter the gang life until 2006. This is just my affiliation with my baby daddy back in 1991–92 and being a part of the gang lifestyle.

I've never been accepted by white people. I don't know who I am. Even in ceremony, sweat lodges, and stuff like that, when you say when you are from, I don't know. Even the Elders that I have met along the way, when I tell them I don't know what I am and I have no clue what I am. However, because of the way I am and the ways I follow, everybody thinks I am Native, you know? I think another reason that I wasn't accepted is because I manipulated that money that I always had access to. I got whatever I wanted, and I got whatever they needed or whatever we needed all the time. Whether it was money, cars, alcohol.

I learned how to manipulate through my parents. I manipulated them for their money. That's where it started. Later I did it through sex, if you will, 'cause I didn't sleep with somebody. You know, what I call prostitution now. I did exactly everything except having sex with them to get what I wanted.

I would only dress up when I needed to manipulate a situation. That's how I used my femininity. I could get whatever I wanted, whenever I wanted, from anyone. The more I watched, the more I witnessed, the more I experienced, the more I got hurt. More and more traumatic things would happen to me that I didn't want to deal with, so I turned to drugs. My life consisted of physical, mental, spiritual, emotional, and sexual abuse, which I thought was normal because that's all I saw around me. I remember waking up every fucking morning to my boyfriend's mom punching his dad in the head, screaming at him, scratching his eyes out. Every morning was him beating the shit out of her because she had the idea in her head that he was cheating on her. 'Cause he was selling drugs out of the milk truck. He would leave at night to go do a drug run, but at the end of it he really was out cheating on her. This all became normal because I spent so much time in that life.

But you see it's not just the Native families that are messed up. My adoptive white middle-class family, who I never thought loved me but really did, they have their own story. It goes back to the churches and priests. It's really fucked up. I sat and talked with my mom for seven hours straight one night on how her life consisted of beatings upon beatings from my adopted grandpa. She was also sexually assaulted and abused by a Roman Catholic priest. When I was younger, she didn't know how to cope with anything, just like me, but she went this way, and I went that way.

Through it all, I wanted my education, and it was one thing I never gave up on. Even though I had bad experiences. Even though I got kicked out of classes and told not to come back. I did, I got my post-secondary on an extended plan. I was the good kid, I was the bad kid, but I looked like the good kid because I was white. Back then, I was the kid that would carry ounces of cocaine. I was the kid that would collect money and not be seen as a criminal. It was all for family, until 2006, that's when I started to sell myself. I think about what they had me doing at the age of fifteen and sixteen, and that's what I had my kids doing, as they were not old enough to get huge charges for it at that time. I ended up graduating high school four days after I had my oldest boy.

After I graduated from grade twelve, I entered a diploma program and opened a day home. So here I am taking care of people's kids during the day and getting high, selling drugs at night. I ended up meeting another guy who I married. He grew up in foster care, group homes and was on his own since he was sixteen. Same kind of lifestyle, except his wasn't street gangs; it was just violence. It was the same background of alcohol, drugs, crime, and criminal records. Then I went to get my education as a child and youth care worker. I excelled top of the class, and before I was even done school, I was offered a job with the provincial government and the public school board.

Again, I am doing that during the day, then I would go home at night to a controlling husband, drugs, alcohol, violence, and just abuse of every kind. Before this, I only smoked weed and drank beer. I stayed away from the dirty drugs because I watched all those people do it and saw what happened to them. I watched how they acted and it scared me. But one night someone offered me a pill, and that was the rabbit hole for me. I took the pill not because I wanted to numb the pain, but because I actually had physical pain in my shoulder. That pill took away all of the other pain as well. After taking it, I didn't have to feel anything anymore, and I could get lost with what was happening around me. It was that pill that led me to gang life and four and a half years of incarceration.

Even though all of this abuse was happening around me, it wasn't happening *to* me. It was happening to the kids that I worked with. To those that I was selling to. But it wasn't happening to me. For some reason, it didn't happen to me, or I thought it wasn't. Going through school with all of this in my mind, I just blocked it out. By the time my eyes said something, my own addiction was spiralling out of control.

I wasn't really a mother to my kids when I was involved in the street. It makes sense to say that I took care of many other people's kids, but I didn't take care of my own because I walked away from them. I left them with my husband or my adoptive mom. I am just learning now how to be a mom. My adopted mom became the mother to my children. She had them on the weekend. I don't know what I would have done without her, because my kids, somewhere along, have morals and values and have stayed out of the life. Except for my oldest daughter.

Then I got a grip on it by talking to others. I did go to rehab but I left and went right back to the same situation. If you don't change everything around you, nothing is going to change.

So when I went back to the street, I was introduced to a crew of Black guys by my street family. They would rent me stuff, and this is where the heavy part of my life on the streets began. That's where the gang I joined came into play. That's where all the crime and robbery really began to escalate. At this time, my husband had seen how deep I was getting and how heavy my using was and he pulled out. He wanted no part of it.

I got approached by a member, and he said, we need to meet. I met with him the same day, within hours of him getting a hold of me. He told me that I was moving stuff through his hood and that he wanted a part of it. He would provide protection for me and my product. From there we were inseparable. He was just like a business partner, a husband on the street as it was always business. We were together like this until we did a bank robbery and he went to jail. I was going to get jumped into the gang one night, but I was pregnant at the time. The girl who was supposed to jump me in didn't, but I miscarried because of all the drug use.

It was soon after that when I took my first crack hoot, and everything began to spiral even more. That hoot had me chasing the dream, just like the pills I took earlier. I couldn't even keep the product long enough to sell it because I was doing it that fast. At the time I was living downtown Regina in a penthouse suite. On my daughter's sixteenth birthday, the cops kicked down the door, and that is how she spent her birthday. I got evicted from there and was too dope sick to function then I was on the streets looking for somewhere to go. All the dope was gone. I had nothing. Just the clothes in my back. I was standing in the lobby of a hotel because they had pay phones. I was calling my husband to see if I could come home and he let me stay one night. Then I went back to detox. I only lasted seven days in there until I went back to the street.

The gang and the street life gave me power. I had control. I was popular. I was accepted. I was loved. I belonged. I was somebody. When I had the drug and was high, I thought the gang was my family. Never in my whole life did I ever feel more accepted than I did then. Believe it or not, a lot of people have trouble believing this, but I am an introvert. I am shy until I build that relationship, where I am comfortable with people.

My whole life I was the...I was the one in the corner watching. I was the one that was never invited anywhere. I was the one that was always picked on. I was the one that was always made fun of, but if I was violent that was cool. Beating up boys on the playground, I was cool. Everything that I actually, I don't know how to say it, I could never feel comfortable in my own skin and wear no masks. I always had to pretend that I was something else to fit in, until now. I didn't know how to deal with all the situations.

I chased that fucking high. I chased it, and there are still days that I want to chase it. I wore and tried to mask my whole life. I masked everything from knowing how I came to be, but also how I came to be on the streets again. I masked everything. The first oxycontin I took was supposed to be for pain for my shoulder because of an accident. Again, it took away the pain. It took away all the fucking pain of my whole life, but it didn't take away my shoulder pain. Then that spiralled to cocaine, to speed balling, to crack, to sticking needles in my arms. All so I didn't have to deal with reality because there was no fucking reality. I was just in my own little world, you know? It wasn't until I was thirty-six years old that I stopped numbing it out.

I know I was nothing but a meal ticket because at the end of the day I plead guilty to thirty-three charges. I took seventeen people's charges, and they didn't force me too, I just did it. I had two Canada-wide warrants for my arrest. We were sitting there, and a lot of them were like, man, I wish I was in on that one. Fuck, she is so solid, this that, blah blah blah. I took everybody's charges, and they all walked with clean slates, except me. For me, I knew I was done and at that point I knew if I didn't plead guilty to thirty-three charges, I was going to die.

I already overdosed five times. I had been strangled to my last breath. Beaten to my last breath. Fucking stabbed, fucking beaten with a hammer. How many times can you get...In one night I was drugged, raped, and robbed for $1,700 and two ounces. I was done. I was fucking done, but obviously, this is the condensed version.

I think back now to when I was a kid, how violent and destructive I was as a kid, how much trouble I would get into and destroy things. I didn't use, but that's how I did it then. Me and my mom have talked about how I was a fucking angry child and nobody could control me. I would have outbursts anywhere. I didn't give a shit. Shoplifting at the age of four, taking whatever. Then I found the drugs and that substituted all of it. Recently though, I have found some supports to try to figure out this healing thing, the proper way without using.

I am still learning. I am not there. My children are grown, going to be twenty-three, twenty-one, sixteen, and live two and a half hours away. My sixteen-year-old only contacts me when he wants something. I owe him because I am a piece of shit. His thinking is that I gave up on him, so I owe him money. Whereas my daughter and other son just want to see me do good. They don't want to ever see me go back. When I do go to visit them, and I have all of them, it's stressful and overwhelming for me. It's like I said to other STR8 UP women, kudos to the female members who go through this and have their kids because I am still learning. For me, it's with my grandkids, right? I want to say I am 75 percent parent because a lot of times I go, and Regina is so overwhelming for me, or it's such a trigger that I just have to focus on staying clean and sober. I have to worry about myself, so I don't go as much as I want. I have an amazing relationship with their "mom." I know she is a foster mom, but I call her mom. That's their mom. She raised them and tried to teach them the good way. They dance pow wow. They go to ceremonies. I can talk to them whenever I want, but I am still learning.

I am still learning, and it's the most amazing feeling in the world. I realize what I do with my grandkids to what

I did or didn't do with my kids. I just shipped my kids off to my mom's; I didn't know. For me now there are so many firsts that I never did with my children.

I am a grandmother, and we celebrated my granddaughter's fourth birthday. In total, I have seven grandchildren. I remember when my granddaughter was being born. My daughter had a pre-arranged C-section. When we went in, I had to go back to her room and get my dope, which I kept in a cupboard to get high. I didn't even go to the hospital the day that they took Jasmine away from my daughter. I never...I held her once. I never saw her again until I got out of jail.

Being a grandmother to me is actually the same role. It's the same role that I play with my kids now, except the difference between my grandkids and kids is my kids don't know me as this person, right? So it's introducing a new person, whereas with my grandkids it's like having my own set of kids, you know? They are all different ages, I incorporate a good way of life and show them positive things. If there are negative things that come up, it's about teaching them there's a way to get through it. When I am with my kids and grandkids, if I am having trouble, I put myself into the position of me being with an Elder and thinking what would they say to me? Or what would they teach me? That's how I guide my grandkids and kids today.

My two oldest grandkids today are in long-term care, but we picked their family. I never worry about them because I know that they are being taught the good way. They're being taught through culture and tradition; I always say they are so blessed to have such a big family that loves them, and how they raise them. Whereas the younger ones are living in the environment where all of the stuff is going on, they see the streets and what they have to offer.

My oldest daughter has been stabbed nine times living the lifestyle. I was not there to witness it happen. I was there after and I visited her. But when you are in the gang life, you never disrespect a man, right? A woman never ever disrespects a man by the way they talk to them, by the things they do. You never hit a man. If you disrespect a man, then you are punished. Everything that's happened to my daughter was a consequence of her mouth or her physically being violent with a man. Back when I was involved, I watched my daughter be held down by three higher-ups, and they were hitting her face because of the way she spoke to me and had no respect for me. Shit like that was just normal. There were consequences for how you acted, and now it's horrifying to think that I ever thought that was normalized behaviour.

Although that happened, I also protected my daughter while I was in the gang. There were lots of times when her boyfriend at the time would get beatings from my bros because of the disrespect for my daughter and me. But then I also think about when you are in a gang, that whole gang is supposed to be your family. The whole of it. I got in at a time where most of the first chapter is now dying, dead, or locked up in the penitentiary. Because of the life and the shit people were seeing and doing, everybody started using, slamming. Their addictions were going out of control; then it was divided. You had to decide which side you were on. I am with so and so, under them and their crew. Or you're on this side and under this crew. It was like they wore the same colours but they fought each other. It was really fucked up, and now there are so many different branches of that. Somebody will throw up, a high-ranking person is there, and I am like who the fuck are you? I don't know.

I have been stabbed. I've been shot at, and it grazed my head. I have been beaten to my last breath, strangled, beaten with a hammer, knocked around, slammed around. The weird thing of all of this is that it never happened to me when my street husband was around. It just didn't happen. He kept me very protected. My daughter has been through way more violence than I have, way more.

Until recently, I said that jail saved my life. I can't answer, jail saved my life anymore. Jail didn't save my life. It was in jail where I found a new way to live and *spirituality* changed my life. I was talking to my parole officer recently, and I am done my sentence soon; but for some reason, in my twisted mind, I think that the very next day everything is going to be gone, and I am going to be back in the game. I know that is not true because I have been given all the tools, lessons, and teachings of how to live a good life. Plus, I am in the system and on parole. It's not me doing it because I was taught a whole new way on how to forgive and deal with all the hurt and pain that we talked about from the beginning.

You see, if we want to work with people who have gone through the same shit as me those who are in social services, addictions counsellors, or anybody else they have to listen. Just hold that space and listen. Half the time, it's not necessary for them to hear something out of you; it's them finding that safe place where it's not going to leave this room where you're not going to be judged. You can get rid of your stuff, and it's not going to go anywhere.

For me, I go every two weeks to see my parole officer and I probably am the only parolee that sits with her parole officer for two hours. But I dump everything I need to. People just need to hold that space, listen, non-judgemental, compassionate, some empathy. Don't tell me you know how it feels; just listen and don't judge. Don't try to fix everything; you can't. Just listen and when I am done, then talk. But don't talk down. Talk as though you are trying to work with me. Don't be a parent figure. I don't need that. *We* don't need that. What we do need are connections and people to listen without judging. Who will help or support us when we need it. In other words, create a safe space, be trusting, non-judgemental, listen, hold space. Every single person loves unconditionally too.

Secondly, not everyone can do everything for one person. I can't go to you for every fucking problem I have; it's not going to work. I would burn you out. So people have to know that we need to create networks of support. That's why I handpick others to help support me.

Third, don't ever fucking feel sorry for me. Why do you feel sorry for me? First of all, you shouldn't feel sorry for me; you should be happy for me because I am here. We're fucking human beings. We have been through shit, made some bad choices and mistakes. But like I said, in the end, if I want the help, I will ask. Oh, if you feel sorry for me, you want to help me. Don't fucking feel sorry and help me unless I ask for it. If I want the help, I'm going to fucking ask for it. If someone is going to offer me, I don't take it. I don't know, that's just me though. There are some people that need to know constantly and have that constant validation that the help is always there. But that's where I leave that. No reason to feel sorry for me.

We all have files who have been in the system. But if you want to help, don't rely on that file to know who I am. Sit and talk. I never read files because I don't care, 'cause everybody has a story. Everybody has been through something and guaranteed whatever is in that file is because of something that is going on in their life. They're hurting. Get to know them as a person, not what is written on paper. Guaranteed what is written on paper is only the bad stuff. There isn't the good stuff.

Open my file, it doesn't say the good stuff. It's all fucking bad stuff. So do you start a relationship based on that? No, just get to know them. Parole officers or bail supervisors, like those types of people, have to write up their reports, they just open their file take all their information based on that shit. They don't sit and have a conversation with you to try and figure out what are your goals and plans. What do you need help with and what would you like to do? Building a relationship and reading a file are two totally different things.

But that is just the way I see it. I don't offer help to anybody unless they ask for it. I will listen and hold space until they are ready. I just listen because I remember when I first got out, there were certain people I went to for help. All I needed them to do was listen, that's it, nothing else. And somehow every time they turned it and made it all about them, and I was like what the fuck? I just need you to shut your mouth and listen. So those that did that I have learned to cross them off the list of people who can help me. How can you help me if you can't stop talking about yourself and what you need today?

That's my life right now. I have love and I have hope. I have a story.

TÂNSI

IT'S GOOD TO BE ALIVE

Jazmyne

I grew up most of my life on a reserve that was next to a small town about three hours from Regina.

I stayed there until I was three years old and then we moved to Saskatoon. It was peaceful out there on the reserve. I only knew Ojibway as I spent most of my time with my grandparents.

My dad did a lot of things. He was a band counsellor, a boxing trainer, hockey coach, and later became the band manager. My mom, she stayed at home with us until I was about eight and then she started going to school for work.

My parents didn't drink or do drugs, nothing. My dad was always working and my mom was home with us. I had three older brothers, a sister, and a half-sister. One of my brothers committed suicide, and both of my sisters have died.

I remember going to a Catholic school in Saskatoon and getting hit because I knew Ojibway. I got bullied from the teachers and the kids because of it. My brother was in an older grade than me and he used to get bullied there too. I wouldn't talk to anybody 'cause, I don't know, I just didn't. Sometimes I couldn't understand what they were saying and I remember the teachers hitting me with a ruler and I was pulled around by my hair. I also remember a deaf girl at the school, this little thing, and she got beaten up and spanked all the time with me because we both couldn't understand. I felt angry and I didn't wanna go to school. So I isolated myself as I was too scared to tell my parents what was going on because the teachers told us not to tell. They said that no one would listen.

When I went to school in Saskatoon, the Indians didn't like me and the whites didn't like me. So it was not fair 'cause I had red hair, and the whites knew I was Aboriginal too, so it wasn't fair. I couldn't fit in anywhere. I remember I was trying to fight back against this one girl when I was in kindergarten who was hitting me. I remember she called me a stupid Indian and I want you to stay away from my sister. And she was laughing at me.

My mom used to be wicked with me. I remember my mom and dad would fight. My mom would try to leave my dad and she would push me away and take care of her other kids. My mom was physically abusive to me when I was a kid.

You know, times when, like...when my brothers or cousins were molesting me and stuff. Like saying it is a secret and trying to touch me and stuff. And she caught one of my cousins one time and she beat me up really bad. I was just a little kid and I didn't know what was going on. I couldn't understand and I so angry with my mom for years. I just couldn't look at her. How could she, the way she treated me...Growing up she didn't have no emotions, she wasn't like a mom...you know, like my dad was really loving. She was so cold. She didn't say I love you. Just cold, you know, she didn't have that kind of emotion and now that I'm older now and I understand 'cause she was in residential school.

Her mother died when she was still a little girl in that school and my grandfather raised her. He was as an alcoholic and was mean to her, so she had no motherly love and no emotions like that 'cause of all the abuse. So it passed down to me. I would pretend she was an evil stepmother and that's how I would deal with her. Today, looking back I can forgive her because of all of this. I don't blame her because she had a tough life, and I am learning to understand it better.

After a while, we moved back to the reserve when I was in grade two and that is where I found out I was Native. I started to go to school in that small town with Indians and white kids. That's how it was. I still remember them playing cowboys and Indians and they would be chasing us around throwing rocks at us and stuff right. It didn't take long for all us Indians got pulled out of school because of the racism that was going. I didn't like the teachers at that town school. The teachers seemed like they hated us for being Indian. I started hating them and not liking teachers. Anyone that had authority, I didn't like them. They made us think that we were lying, you know, for telling what they were doing. This one teacher wrote an article in school about the Indians being cows and that. My dad was the education director for the reserve and he pulled all the kids out of the school and started our own school on the reserve.

But it was after all this that I started turning into a bully when I moved back to the rez and started school on the reserve. I wouldn't listen to my mom anymore. I would fight her now for hitting me. So I started fighting back. Just not listening anymore. I didn't want to listen. There was a...I used to get into fights all the time. I was getting tired of getting being beaten up.

I used to feel so dirty to be an Indian when I was young. You know, the white girls would be saying "ew" when they saw me and others. They would be like that, but I always wanted to be like them. I used to think girls go to ballet, are princessy, and I couldn't be like that. I grew up with boys, played hockey, and as I got older...my dad was so tired of me being picked on he started to train me as a boxer. He started training me to fight back and...that's where I started getting an aggression. I was watching other kids, watching the white kids, TV shows and stuff like that, and that's what got me starting to fight back.

I started to fight back and bully others when I was twelve and that's when I started to feel empowered. The power that I was someone. I was starting to be somebody. I started to get noticed finally. I started to get friends and started to fit in somewhere. I'd fit in with the bad asses. I started getting in trouble, smoking cigarettes, stealing, experimenting with drugs, inhalants, alcohol, and stuff like that when I was thirteen. When I was fourteen I ended up in a young offender centre for beating up a girl. This is where I met up with a guy who was a bully and everyone was afraid of him. I thought that he was a cool guy and I always wanted to hang around him.

I didn't fit in anywhere, except with bad kids after this point. I started listening to rap music. I used to wear baggy clothes and breakdancing, bad guys were all in. They were cool to me and I wanted to be part of them, too. But the thing is that I was such a bully. I was only with friends because I was a bully and I was always the one with the money. I paid for everything and then they were trying to use me. And I freaked out on three of them and beat them all up. And I got charged again because one of them went through with the charges. After that the older boys, they would call me Mike Tyson and I started to feel cool and have a reputation...but I ended up going to jail because of it at fourteen.

You know, like, even though I was like bad and stuff, I still did my ceremonies and went to feasts and that. Doing ceremonies and trying to be good but being bad at the same time. After that time, that was when I started running with a gang. That's when it really all started for me, when I was in the youth facility.

Before my time in YO [young offender facility] I didn't know gangs existed. I didn't know nothing like that. It felt like a stellar movie when I cliqued in. You know, I just thought gangs were a TV/movie thing like *Blood In Blood Out*. When I was there too, the guys there were talking to me and I didn't think I was pretty or I was beautiful. I had little self-esteem. At the time, I don't know,

beautiful girls would wear makeup and fix themselves up. Dressed in dresses, you know, and I didn't do that.

I hated everybody in the facility. I was so angry and blaming everyone for being there. So pissed off at everyone. I remember going in there I was so mean. We were sitting in this little cell with this girl we were getting ready to be shipped off to go to court and they started singing and I was like, be quiet, man, and she told me no. I beat the shit out of her right there.

Then all these other girls that were hanging out with gang guys started noticing me for my toughness. After that, us girls started cliquing. I was always angry looking where I always had this mean look. It was just a big front where I acted crazy, that I would do anything to hurt you, to get away from you. But I was hurting inside and I didn't feel love for anybody, only my dad.

But being with the gang I felt cool because I thought all the gang guys that I was starting to hang out with were cool. They all looked after each other and that they were all tough people. Tough guys. Anything happens to one, they would all jump in. I hung around them a lot but I didn't join until I was in my mid-twenties. That's when it actually happened.

After YO, I went home back to my family where I started to learn about street life from by oldest half-sister, who taught me how to be like a woman. She had a different mother than me but we looked exactly like each other, but she was seven years older, but we were real close. She grew up different from me, though. She grew up with her mom, and her mom was on the streets. But her life rubbed off on me and she became a role model. She taught me how to use guys for money. It was on the reserve and the street life, you know, her mom partying and bringing home all these different men. My sister, she got molested and raped really young, too. They lived poor as there wasn't any food in the fridge and then she'd have to go prostitute herself to feed her family and stuff like that. Her mom used to make her go out in the streets as she was addicted to pills.

She even sold my sister to doctors and stuff to get pills, and she was about eleven when this happened. And I ended up knowing everything like that.

We used to drink and smoke up together all the time and do pills once in a while. She started helping me to understand being a woman, you know? She used to say, "Oh, dress like this, dress like that." She was telling me, "Oh, stop acting like a boy," and that I should show off my body more and stuff

like that. I learnt how to be a girly girl, wearing makeup and stuff. My sister started teaching me how to go to bars to get shit paid for, and how to steal this and that. I would use men, calling them dumb and everything. I was using my looks to get what I wanted. I started to dress how she taught, to fix myself up, fix my eyebrows and my hair. I would mostly go for the guys that had very high self-esteem and had money. I was also prostituting myself out, but I kept all of the money myself. This was all in Saskatoon, before I got pregnant with my first son at nineteen.

When I found out that I was pregnant, I quit everything. I left the father, and left everybody to go back to the reserve to be with my parents because I wanted them to help me. I wanted to have a healthy baby, so I just quit everything and went home. I settled down for a bit. I was sober for two years and was going to school. At this time, I had my son, a house, and my own car. When I was younger, I always wanted a family. A father, a baby, to be a wife, you know, what everyone wants. But the guy who I got pregnant with was married. He already had a wife, he just had a baby like three weeks before I found out. So I ended up been a single mom and I did everything for my baby. I was sober for, like, two years. I just figured it on my own. I did everything for my baby.

I was single for a long time and then I ended up going out with the wrong guy, and we both started using drugs and alcohol. I started smoking up again. That was the first guy I ever lived with in my life. That guy was mean to my son, but he would do it behind my back. I'd find bite marks and bruises on him. He ended up cheating on me all the time, and he used to hit me too. I don't know, he was just another guy that ruined my life.

He really messed me up. I fell in love with that guy and I ended up drinking all the time. My dad would always have my son and was like, "That's the little boy I dreamt of." He said, "When he's two years old I'm gonna keep him. I'm gonna look after him. I'm gonna teach him everything I know."

I remember how angry I was at that guy. I did everything for him. He didn't even try to work or try get on welfare, nothing! He'd live off me and he was mean to my baby, he cheated on me all the time, stealing off me, using me. He made me feel like nothing. I didn't know what to do because I still had low self-esteem. I thought I was so ugly and a terrible person, you know? I was so angry. I went to go visit my sister in Regina, and we were drinking and we just kept on drinking. My little nieces

were just babies at that time, my little son was a baby, but my dad had him.

One time we were driving to Saskatoon, and we were drunk all the way from Regina. We were driving in my car and she just start coming out about her mom. How her mom didn't like me and I was yelling at her that her mom broke up my home. She got mad and punched me. So we had a really big fight. We were just crying so I stopped fighting and just let her beat the shit out of me. She was just hurt and it came out how she felt, how she was jealous of me and my dad. I really loved my sister and that's the only time we ever fought. So I left Saskatoon and went back home. One day I got a call early in the morning from my stepsister's cousin telling me that my stepsister had overdosed and that I needed to call the hospital. Her mom didn't want me or my dad at the funeral because she blamed us for her death, but I ended up going to the funeral anyways. I found out later that she died because she took someone else's methadone and had a massive heart attack, where she collapsed on the bathroom floor. See my sister never did needles, but she was always trying to get high, to get away from her anger. She left two little girls and I still have contact with one of them. It still makes me sad thinking about it. How she was constantly selling her body, selling crystal meth while she was on it, but she was a really pretty and smart girl, just a lot of hurt and anger.

I was really angry after my sister died. I used to blame myself over what happened, over her dying, you know? I had to put up with that anger. So I would just go and beat up people, and started to get back to who I was before.

I was twenty when I first went to Pinegrove. I did a home invasion 'cause I just wanted to prove myself. I was with my boyfriend's dad's girlfriend and she was talking smart to me, and she owed me money. I got charged because she pissed me off and I punched her out. I got fourteen months, conditional. About a month before my sentence was to start, I started to hang out with that old crew from my youth again.

When I ended up going to the correctional, I saw my cousins and I thought it was a big joke. I didn't take my life seriously. I thought it was so funny. I didn't know what I was doing to myself and I didn't care. I ended up getting out early 'cause they were just gonna ban smoking from Pinegrove and they were afraid of a riot, so they were sending out all the short timers, so they sent me out right away. After that, that's when I started getting connected again, drinking, partying. I ran into old guy friends and started going back into my old ways. Like I started robbing and stuff, and I didn't care, I just kept drinking and drinking all the time. When I went to Regina to do pick-ups, I would run into the old gang members and buy drugs off of them to sell on the reserve.

I soon met my other baby's daddy. When I met him, he was after me and I was just out there to use him for a party. I got pregnant off him, people always asked why we were together and I would tell them that he had money and he was gonna do this and that. But when I got pregnant, he tried to leave me right away. I ended up back on a bracelet again because of that home invasion. So I just stayed home. I was done getting into trouble after I did the time with the bracelet, and finished my conditional, you know, and I thought I wouldn't go back in court no more, but I was still drinking and stuff. I was still partying as my baby daddy went from a nice guy that would do anything for me to a real asshole trying to control me after the baby was born. I would have somebody visiting me, a friend, cousin, anyone, and he would get mad. He wouldn't want me to have friends or any of my family over. He just started turning into a controlling person. His other baby mamma called and told me to be careful, that he was abusive and controlling, but I didn't listen. My dad got a bunch of money and he bought a house for me and the kids to move into. So we did, we moved in there, and yeah I ended up having my baby with him and we stayed together. The only thing I couldn't stand about him is he would just up and leave, he wouldn't help me with my son.

When I was with my new baby daddy, that's when I started getting into trouble again, because of him. He would hit me and beat me up and then he would call the cops on me. He had this little manipulating attitude where he pretended that I was crazy and that he never did anything to me. I always got charged and I couldn't even tell the cops that he'd hit me all the time. I remember this one time he went out drinking. I was thinking, well, fuck you, if you are going to treat me like this, I'm gonna go out partying with somebody else. Anyways he came back after three days and he kicked me in the face while I was trying to breastfeed my son. I was bleeding on my baby. My baby was crying he was just a little guy. He grabbed me by my head and I fell with my baby and he beat me up. He was kicking me in the face. He then went running to the police right after and said he wanted to charge me for assault. So when the cops came over they charged me. We had restraining orders on each other, but I loved him

and I hated him at the same time, so it was hard. I was trying to keep my family together and I ended up having my daughter soon after.

I had no one to protect me from him. When I would call the cops I would get arrested. But if I had a black eye or a shoe print on my face, I would still get arrested because I wouldn't cooperate with them. Because I wouldn't tell what he was doing to me, so I ended up getting incarcerated because of him. That's when I started getting down in the gang, because I was promised all of this stuff. I was going to be protected from him because I wanted him hurt, because he hurt me so much. He almost killed me a few times and I wanted him scared. I wanted him to feel what I felt, so I joined. So I get down and the beatings stopped. He stopped hitting me. He knew what was going on. I couldn't call to help me, they wouldn't listen to me. They listened to him. So I found a way to protect myself.

To be part of something is another reason I wanted to join. Because I was really abused by my kids' dad and he always got away with everything and I was, I ended up getting charge for him beating me up, you know? And I wanted him to hurt, I wanted him to suffer, and I knew if I was part of a gang he would stop hating me.

So I cliqued up with a gang. It was a sign of power being with this gang. Seeing the tags in the neighbourhoods, it was like a sense of belonging somewhere. So when I saw somebody disrespecting the tags, I got mad. It was a pride thing.

I also joined up because I always thought it was so cool, from movies and stuff. But I was also into the bad boy thing, you know? When I was in the gang I didn't have to dress up or try to make myself look pretty like I did earlier. I got power from the gang and a thrill out of being in it. I thought that I was, you know, high and mighty.

Usually if I did dress up all sexy and stuff, I would go out down to the stroll and learn tricks, go and make some money. I was mostly robbing. I didn't want to have sex with anybody. If I was drunk enough, high enough, I would, but if I wasn't, I wouldn't do anything like that. I was addicted to that life. I was addicted to drunks and I was addicted to the party life, addicted to the attention from men, the way they would look at me.

I saw all the guns and that, but I never ever seen anybody get shot at or never seen a drive-by. I have got guns held up to me, you know, and stuff like that, and been a part of home invasions. There isn't much of a difference of having a gun pulled on you and a home invasion. They are both pretty much the same. I had the gun pulled on me by bikers and it had nothing to do with me, it was with my ex at the time. It was because of him doing shit to bikers at that time and they pulled guns out on us, surrounded our car and one biker had a shotty [shotgun] on me. He was holding it on me because my ex robbed from one of their guys. I was just sitting there, I was scared. I looked at him and told him to kill me, that if he did I would haunt him as a ghost and told him that I would see him in hell. You know, that's how I was talking to him and he laughed at me and told me to get out. So I got out and he pushed me away from the car, telling me that he never wanted to see me again and dragged me away. I never seen them ever again.

I was going to get a patch like that one day and that was how I was going to keep making money. I thought it looked cool to be a gangster. It wasn't what I expected it to be. After all the people I lost, that died, I would take pills to calm myself down because I lost a lot of people. I couldn't do needles though, had to do with stitches or something.

The gangs are getting younger and worse because they are using weapons. It's worse because everybody loves their kids. Everybody wants them to do well and then you send them to school in hardcore neighbourhoods learning from other kids. Then they think that the gang is the thing to be in to be cool and to think you're a part of something, you know? Why would you want to be involved these days?

Now it's all different. It's just young kids. I looked at pictures of gangs on the internet in Saskatoon, here, and there are little wee kids starting to be in gangs. I see them walking around with their flags, you know, thinking that is something it because they want people to fear them. Younger kids now, mine are vulnerable, they will think that they're in with something. That they have a little sense of power because they are a part of something and want to run everything. That's how it goes. It's sad now. That is why I get scared for my kids and they are on a reserve now.

I was talking to two thirteen- and fourteen-year-old boys, and one of them is going to be a dad and both of them are in a gang. Both know how to cook up oil and crack. The conversation made me think. I am just so grateful for where my kids are right now because of what they are doing. How good they are doing. My boys are playing hockey, one has his licence, and following Native ways, doesn't do drugs. Makes me thankful for where my children are. Makes me think of how I was when I was younger.

Fear was important for change for me because I didn't want to be another piece of "garbage," as one guy put it to me. To be forgotten or another missing Indian woman, that is what made me think because I have children. If their mom is missing, would they find me buried somewhere? I didn't want my kids to have a...who wants their mom dead, missing and forgotten? Nobody wants that for their mom. That's how ashamed I was of myself. That's when I decided I had enough; I don't want to live like that no more.

I remember this one time I was roommates with this chick and she stole money off this guy and blamed me. At the time I was trying to work and live the life. I was trying to do both, have a job and sell drugs to make quick cash. Anyways, I was walking home and he said I ripped him off and these three girls come and start fighting me. I started fighting back and they had a hard time beating me up, right? He comes and he punches me really hard and pulls out a knife. He then starts chasing me over three hundred dollars, and then he said that I was going to go missing and nobody would give a shit about me. He said that the cops won't look for me, that they don't care. That nobody cares if Native women went missing then.

It is really, really hard, it's true, though. There have been times where I was afraid of the police to even talk to them, you know? I don't know, it's hard. I always had a hard time with police, you see, 'cause when I would get beat there by my husband it would be turned on me, so I began to see them as not caring, they didn't care what happened to me, or people like me. But it's happened more than just with him. The first time, I was sixteen years old and I ran away. I was raped by some creep who ended up getting let go. The cops then put it on me saying that I was dressed like this and that I made myself vulnerable, basically that I was asking for it. So they let the guy go.

The guy who raped me was Indigenous and he got away with it, yet I got locked up running to them for help. They locked me up with some woman who just murdered some people. That is who they locked a runaway with. Someone who just murdered two people. She could have hurt me in that cell. Why would they do that to me, me being vulnerable?

So yeah, it was like this in Regina, but also all over the place. I swear, all over the place. There are so many women who don't want to say anything because they are afraid. That they are not going to listen. That they are not going to help you with what you're saying, with what you're supposed to do. So they turn it around and put it on the girls.

I remember another time where my cousins were fighting and my other cousin called the cops. So one cop sends my little cousin into the car first and then me, and tells me that he wanted to check me for weapons. That I was to hold my arms out. So I held my arms out and he touched me in a really ugly way, and I didn't know what to do. What was I supposed to do? If I reacted, he would have charged me. I just had to stand there and let him touch me like that. My cousin was just shaking in the car watching. Then he was holding me [sniffling], telling me not to "flinch, baby." He couldn't do anything wrong [crying]. I couldn't do anything to him or flinch. I just let him touch me like that. He then let us go after that, after he dropped us off.

Whether the day will come where we will be remembered. Those that are gone don't have a lot of connections when they are on the streets, unless they are cliqued up. But again it's pretty much all the same, we are just Indian women. We know, as Indian women, that we are easy targets to be taken away or go missing. If it is white woman, or any other race, the cops will try to find them right away. But when it is an Indian, they just think it is another woman on the street, just another prostitute, so they are supposed to go missing. It's awful. I thought I was going to be someone like that, to be forgotten.

I was looking for something. Looking for a miracle. A way to stop and get out of it. What the hell was I doing to myself? I was just running back to jail, hospital. I thought that I was forgotten about. My mother doesn't love me. I can't see my kids. I would think about all of that, but I would always end up back on the streets. I was completely stuck between two worlds of being good and bad and not understanding, you know?

People don't understand, they have a one-track mind, and they look down on people. I don't think there is any such thing as bad; it's called healing, you know? It is starting to fix yourself inside your heart, you know? You just got to keep doing it, that's all I got to say.

When I was actually living on the streets, I was out of the gang. I still was still hanging with some of them, you know? I don't know how to explain it trying to be good, trying to be in still. Too used to one way of living, I guess. It's tough, though, trying to get out of it while still living the lifestyle, doing drugs, stealing, and hanging around with people that are still heavily into their addictions, too.

I don't really see a difference between trying to get out of the street life, living on the streets, and getting out of the gang life. They are pretty much the same. I didn't see as being a gang member. I always thought I was on those TV shows or like those music videos with pimps, big guys on 'roids, bling, and all of that money. But it wasn't that. It was living poor. So we leaned on each other, you know, to live. It is a different life.

There's not really a difference to living on the streets and being a gang member. Most of them are poor. They get out of jail and they don't know how else to live. Some people don't know how to work outside of the streets or get stuff for themselves. They end up back there, homeless, and nothing to show for themselves. It's a life that I thought was something else. Where you think it's something else. A life where you think you have a lot of money, it's cool and all of this, but it's not like that.

Like I said, culture is a big thing for me. It always has been. But a lot of traditional people that are in gangs, you see them. You know people who are part of gangs still go to church and all that stuff too, right. And when we saw rivals at cultural events, you wouldn't do anything. You just acknowledged that you see them and leave it till later. So I would always go back to the reserve, to my family, to ceremonies when I was in trouble. I still am today. I still go back for ceremony. There are so many times that I can say I went back so I could go away in ceremonies. But then I would end up going back and getting into more trouble. But nobody is perfect and everybody makes mistakes, and I can always go back to my culture, vent it out there by praying. I am not an assimilated Indian; I know the culture. My addiction kept dragging me away, though. But it wasn't just that. It was about wanting to fit in and having fun like everybody else and I was all alone. You see that no one is really there with you.

My boyfriend now he accepts me for who I am. He knows that I did that, the stuff that I did. I never hid nothing about my past [sniffling]. There are so many times [sniffling], so many times I was used and just left alone. I put boundaries up to protect myself. Before I just let it happen, many times. Because I can say that I got raped so many times that I can't count and I don't like it. I don't like that attention anymore like I use to like it, you know? I woke up so many times and there would be a guy having sex with me and not know who he is. So I would just drink, and drink and drink and do drugs and just to hide that shame... those feelings. My boyfriend now is not out to hurt me, and I know that. He is not there to do that to me. He is not there to use me. He respects me. He loves me. He knows that there is hope for me to change. He stands right there with me. He knows what I have been through.

Faith

I remember growing up in the US we had a big white picket fence and a dog that guarded us. Our dad was overprotective because drug dealers lived right next door. So we had a big old high fence so nobody could look at us and we couldn't get out.

I grew up a Christian. Before my dad became a Christian, he was well known as a thug, and everybody was scared of him. He was crazy and known as a sniffer. He drank heavy and would constantly be the deadliest person wherever he was. Everybody was scared of him. The reason we were Christian is because he stopped in a church one night and he was gonna kill himself. He went in there and said he felt love for the first time. You see, he never felt that because he was raised in an orphanage. After that night, he turned to Christianity. He then came to Canada and met my mom. My mom at the time was all over the place because her mom was dead. She died in a house fire when my mom was five months old.

In the orphanage, my dad was molested. My mom was also molested. It was because of this that they tried to protect us kids. They did a really good job, there were good things, and there were bad things, like all families, but they kept it together as best they could. They tried to give us everything when we were kids. We had the first TV, a big floor TV, a record player, we didn't know how to use it, but we had one. It was what people would call normal because we had everything, but we were isolated.

My parents would travel all over the United States. We had a lady living with us who would look after us. I remember some bad things and some good things during this time. I remember my dad getting mad at my mom and throwing a cup at us. It just missed us, and hit the glass. I don't know what they were mad about, but we knew to stay in the room.

I grew up in a white town in the US. I didn't know we were the only Aboriginals in the town. When we went into town, I remember my mom always standing up for us, but I didn't know why. I just remember her never backing down and making sure we were okay. At the white school, the white teachers would treat us differently. They believed that all Native Americans had head lice so we got sent home. My mom just went marching up there pissed off. When my

mom came there, she was just wicked to get her point across saying we were individuals as much as the other white students. The teachers apologized and told her that it was just dandruff.

In grade three, I remember another teacher centering me out. She said, "Did you know that you're an Indian? Look at your skin and look at Peggy's skin." It's grade three, and I was there to learn, but she made me compare my arm to the white student. She said, "Look at you, do you think you're white? You're not white. You come from a tribe; you have long hair, you're not what you think you are, you were given your name. You don't even know your real name. You don't know who you are. A chief probably gave you your name; your last name is probably not even your own," she told me. I didn't tell my mom, but I did try to make my skin white.

I got white cover-up, and put it all over myself, but it didn't work. I was just so white, and it was just funny. Me and my other friends were trying to get white because there were maybe two other Indians in that class. We thought that Javex would work if we scraped it on our skin. So we tried Javex, but it just burnt the shit out of our skin.

I remember that people in town called Natives "savages who killed and scalped people." I remember listening to that in history. We were separated from the white kids in school 'cause we got tested on. All of the Native kids would have to go in the locker room, and they would put a steel thing on their back to make sure they don't have a crooked back. They said "all Natives have crooked backs." It would hurt, clamp down on our skin, and put our hands out. I just hated doing that.

One day when I was in grade four or five I was in the school bathroom washing up, looking at my long hair in the mirror and these girls came in there and started fighting me. They piled up on me. They were pulling me by the hair and whatnot. I fought back, but I got in trouble. I got detention, and had to write a hundred sentences saying that I will not fight during school hours. I was trying to tell the truth, and they didn't even...I was just standing there, I really didn't know how to fight. I had heard my parents argue, but I didn't know people actually fought each other.

After that, I knew I had to be sneaky because nobody was going to listen to me even if I told the truth. So I was sneaky. I learned to lie. I learned to get revenge, and, man, I got those bitches back. I got them back. I felt so frustrated, sitting there, and I could see those girls taunting me. I was sitting there and I remember thinking, why tell the truth? The truth doesn't even get you anywhere. My parents raised me to tell the truth, and that I'll be okay if I told the truth. Then sitting there after I got beat up, I decided to say, fuck the truth. I ain't gonna tell the truth. I gotta be sneaky, fast. Then I understood why my dad was teaching me all that stuff.

At the age of nine, my mom knew that my father was cheating on her. She was depressed, and didn't wanna lose her marriage and split our family apart. She didn't want people to talk about her in this way. She thought her only way out was suicide. One day she yelled at all of us to stay in the house during our daily walk. She said, "I'm walking by myself." And she went by herself. Twenty minutes maybe passed and I felt in my heart that she was not coming back. I went running for her after I made sure my siblings were settled 'cause they listened to me. I went running for about a mile, and I still couldn't see my mom. I ran towards the railroad tracks and the grid road I still didn't see my mom and I was getting worried. I remember crying even more because I just couldn't see my mom and this was the way she usually goes. So I just remember running and crying. Crying my eyes out yelling for her and out of nowhere she pops up. She was in the side of the ditch in some tall trees. She showed herself on the road.

I went running to see her, and she was crying. I was just nine years old, and she had this rope, she was gonna put it on the tree and kill herself. She yelled at me to stand and watch for cars. I remember a car coming. I ducked down in the grass, and so did she. She got back up, and she had that rope, and I remember she was behind me. I don't know what she was doing, but it broke, and then my mom just started crying like this big, deathly cry. She couldn't kill herself. I was going to throw the rope away, but she told me to hold onto it.

We walked to the trading post, slowly talking. We sat on a hill, and she said, "Faith, no matter what happens, always look after your sisters, no matter what." I just knew then that love was just gonna kill people. After that day I did not want to love anybody because I saw how love was killing my mom. My dad was cheating on her right in front of her eyes, and because of how she was raised she wanted to keep her family together. She never had a family growing up, and I understood that part when I got older. I didn't understand right away. That's when the whole entire world just turned around for me. My dad started going on anti-depressants, he would sit on the couch and sleep. He wouldn't even talk to us anymore. So we just learned how to have all the duties done because

dad wasn't gonna mind us anymore. My mom was gone now, and he would just sit there. He did tell me one time that if I ever heard his gun go off to call the ambulance. I sat in the dark basement by myself waiting for it to go off. He was gonna kill himself. But it didn't go off, and my dad banged on the floor. I went upstairs, and he hugged me. He was crying, telling me he was sorry and then I remembered again that love was gonna kill everybody, so don't love anybody. See, a short time later my cousin was hanging in the basement for three days. He hung himself, and he was in the basement for three days. I saw his body getting taken out. It was all swollen and fat. Love killed him too.

Love is death.

With all of this, growing up, I didn't even know what a girl was supposed to be. I wasn't trained like other little girls. My little sisters were trained like princesses, where they got their hair fixed, got to play and live freely. I didn't. I was trained military style, where I had to run, do errands, and get everything done. I was a good housecleaner. I fixed my bed properly. I knew how to straighten things out, and how to get things done. Instructions were not a problem for me.

I didn't have a role model, but when the cops are always at your door, and you're known as the shit kids or the kids that are always doing something wrong, then you know who you are supposed to be. As I got older, around twelve gangsters from Minneapolis came to our town. We learned to be very manipulative and nobody fucked with us. My older brother, a friend, and I used to always play guns. We always wanted to be Crips because that was the biggest gang down in the United States then. We would hang out at Lisa's, who became my role model. She let us smoke cigarettes, load and clean the guns. She would buy us cigarettes, and we would do everything there.

One guy from Minneapolis was telling us about the Crips, the Latin Kings, the Disciples, the Folk, and he was showing us a bunch of gang signs. The guy was a little bit older than us, like thirteen, fourteen. That's when we knew we all wanted to be gangsters because when you're that young, and you don't know where the fuck you belong, you'll take it. By this time, the kids who all hung out together, most of our families, were split up. He said that our group would be our new family, one that could not be taken away from us, as long as we helped each other, and had each other's back. Before we were just colours, but now we were a family. We all slept together, we all ate together, we all ran together. If somebody cried, we were there for each other.

We had to take a minute to get in. We would be blood brothers and sisters forever. Nobody could take that away from us.

Later, when I had my own kids, I taught them how I was taught. I showed them how to be quick and street smart. I wanted to make sure my kids would be protected. One night I got in a fight with my oldest's dad. I don't know if he kicked me, punched me, or something else but right after I gave birth to my oldest daughter, who was rushed to NICU [newborn intensive care unit]. I remembered because of the fight something happened, and I didn't get to hold her right away.

When I did get to hold her, I sat there in a rocking chair, and she had those little things for her heart monitor. The nurses took her out of the incubator, she was doing good, breathing well, and her heart was good. I remember just holding her in the rocking chair, and I said to her, "I don't know what this world's gonna hold for you when you grow up, but I'll teach you everything that I know so that you can make it." And I remember just looking out the big window. I knew she was so innocent, but I knew the lifestyle, it was gonna be rough. Then I kissed her on her forehead. Nobody even came to visit me till later. Her dad showed up. As soon as he showed up, he peeked around the corner because he knew I was pissed off.

Over time, I made my own name. I moved to cities with SE. I wasn't like the others as I wasn't a part of a family like everybody else. Remember I lived in the US and now I am in Canada, so I had to make my own name. Early on I was the girl from the US, but now it's me and my daughter. SE's childhood was mostly about running away and hiding. She learnt how to be quick since she could walk.

To be quick is like if I was fighting with my partner at the time, I'd say "hurry up!" and I knew she'd be downstairs ready to go. She'd be standing at the front door waiting for me. That was at two years old. That's just before I got tortured for a whole day by my partner. That time I got a phone call out to my one friend, she was a white lady, and I asked her to get SE out of there ASAP. She came up in time, grabbed her, and took her just right before the doors locked. I never saw SE for two days after that.

I wanted to be a good mother, like, having three square meals because I came from a home like that, where we had everything. So I knew what it was and I just wanted her to have everything that I did when I was a kid, but it wasn't possible. So SE grew up around a lot of gangsters, violence, dysfunction, but really...It was poverty.

When you're a young mother like me, I was seventeen just turned eighteen when I had SE, shit, you don't know what the hell to do. When you don't have money to buy anything, you find ways to not face reality because you're not able to support yourself or others. And if you want to go to school, you're questioned by the teachers and social workers when something happens. "Why are you late? Why is this happening?" For me I was like, "Why can't you just shut the fuck up? You know I'm trying here." My social worker told me that I was a bad mom. I didn't know that at the time it was because of poverty. At this point in my life, I didn't see myself as anything because I didn't even know I had an identity. So I thought I'm just gonna raise SE how I was raised, military style.

After these encounters, I became even more filled with rage, which I used to protect SE. I would stomp up anybody if they hurt my baby. I always tried to protect my kids because I never felt protected from my parents after those earlier things. I vowed when I got older that I would never let my babies feel like they were never protected or like they couldn't come to me. SE knows that she can come to me if anything happens. She knows that I'm just like a raging lunatic to everyone, nobody can stop me. Not even my mother or sisters can stop me. They know when I'm mad everybody just moves. And I'll look for any weapon, thinking about slicing up somebody if anybody hurts my babies.

I watched SE's actions as she grew and she wasn't stupid. I knew to trust her if she's going down in the hood. I knew that she would be okay when she was in the hood. You see we were walking one time, a rival gang rolled up, and I had her with me. I told her that these girls were going to fuck us up, and I am going to stash you for a bit. So I stashed her, and she stayed there. I told her not to move or make a sound. So she stayed there for a bit, and I went to go check it out. I came back when it was all clear, and I told her to remember that the light attracts dumb people. Always stay in the dark alleys because nobody's gonna look in dark alleys because they're scary. Stay in the shadows. So I taught her to walk in the shadows of dark alleys.

Whatever I told her to do, I always made sure she had everything. She always knew to keep a weapon. This is stupid now that I look back on it. But when she was young, I taught her to never slice up the right side of someone 'cause that's your main artery. I told her that if you have to stab somebody stab them in the leg, in the thigh or slash them a bit. That scares the shit out of them I told her. It was dumb to teach her, but...I didn't want nothing to happen to her. I didn't want her to ever feel helpless no matter what.

Because when that guy beat me up when I was a teenager, I thought he was some shit. Like I thought he was gangster because he's been in the pen and did this and that. Everybody was scared of him on the streets, but once he did that, it made me realize, you know, you can't trust anybody, not even the toughest gangster. So I said, fuck that shit, I'll never ever let my kids feel vulnerable to predators or anything like that. That is another reason why I taught them how to protect themselves.

My oldest son was taught how to "keep six!" and shit. Who the hell— you know, he's just this little boy and knows keep six. He knows everything. He knows about the cops. He knows to keep the kids quiet. He lives with his adopted dad, and that's where he's at right now. I don't get along with his adopted dad, 'cause he thinks I set him up because he was in a rival gang and got sliced up pretty bad a little while back. I said, "Fuck, man, I don't even run that life. Why would I get you sliced up? Everybody knows you're my baby's dad; nobody's gonna touch you."

Like my daughters, I tell my son there's men out there that are predators too. They'll grab you and do shit to you. They would say, "Holy shit, mom. Weird, rank." I said, "Well, I have to tell you the realities and the truths of the streets, nobody gives a fuck out there."

I would never give them hope for the streets. They needed to be the one that's always in power and control. That's what I tried to instill in them. That's what I did instill in them. At the age of nine, my oldest boy knew how to do bro hand-shakes, he knew everybody on the streets, and he was just a little boy! He had his other cousins and little friends; if they wanted drugs or anything, they would ask my son. He knew, and he wasn't stupid, man. As long as he knew how to take care of himself, didn't get himself killed or in a predicament, I was okay with it.

I didn't understand; I could never understand why I was chosen to be in this kind of darkness. How could I get out of it? How could I show my kids that we have nothing, but still have every-thing? Like I said, I passed down the things I was taught growing up, that no matter what, there's always a way out.

Back when I was repping, I would look to find the girls that were like me, tough mentally and physically. The other ones that try to act all gangster, I would just make them my friends so they could do everything. Clean my house or clean my yard. I don't even remember that many of the gang girls at that time, there wasn't girls in the gang I joined because I just remember all the boys, this is like in '96 and '98, remember. That's more or less when the gang started, so it was fresh and the beginning of it was in '92 or '94.

That was just the beginning of it, you know, all the girls, or all the thug wives, I guess you could say. They're always beaten up, man. I remember my sisters always having black eyes, coming to stash at my house. That was the beginning of a frickin' vicious cycle. I remember all of them always getting beaten up. I was grouchy to them, too. Back then, if the women were dumb, I'd be like, "What the fuck you looking at?" My twin sister looks really mean, and they knew I had a twin. I'd be standing there, she's way bigger, and I'd be like, "What are you fucking looking at?" Everybody would say, "Nothing!" Back then, the ones that wanted to come in...I remember hearing stories that some of them are running away from foster homes. Some wanted to get away from step-parents or uncles molesting them. That's when I'd say you can come stay at my house. I guess I was like a mother figure, holy shit.

I remember one time I had a whole bunch of teenage girls at my house. I think there were four or five. I would feed them, and they would have a safe place to sleep. In return, I had their loyalty, and they would do anything for me. This one time, I don't know who got beat up, but it was one of my good sisters. I told the girls that were staying with me to go fuck 'em up, and I would be watching to make sure they did it. We went walking to that block, and the girl that fucked up my sis answered the door. I remember they ripped the door screen off, dragged her out, and just gave her a dirty licking. I remember standing over her telling her to never touch any of my girls again.

I kept the house neat, so everybody liked our house. We lived in a three-storey house that everybody liked. They loved coming over. I knew how to keep order. That's why I never got bossed around by chicks even when I was deep in. I remember when I got older, I was wearing a jersey, and it had maroon on it. One homegirl was chilling, saying that I was wearing red. I told her to fuck off and that I could do whatever I wanted or wear whatever colour I wanted. It wasn't even red, and they're trying to say I was chilling with a rival gang. But they were jealous because they weren't working. If we gave them work, they would just

slam it up anyways. But I think they lacked self-confidence in who they were.

It was really hard for the women as some wouldn't be treated right. If they had a baby, I would help them out or whatever. Who your baby dad is really depends on how you were treated. I can only speak for myself because when my baby was born, they picked up my baby put a bandana and a gold chain around him. They were cruising him around in the hood.

My one son's name is spelled like Syndicate and Loyalty 'cause his dad's handle was Loyalty. His dad is a well-known gangster, and my baby was treated like royalty. His godparents are sitting in the penitentiary right now. They are big-time gangsters. They still acknowledge my son in the pen, every-where, and everybody knows he is treated different from my other kids.

Like I said, I have five baby dads, and I quit caring after my oldest boy. I love my babies with all my heart, but I quit caring like, "Oh, I'm having a baby! Oh, this is what's gonna happen!" I stopped caring because the dads didn't care or anything. I was by myself. I learned that nobody was gonna fucking be there for me and I was nineteen at this time. So my next baby I was happy, but I didn't tell nobody. Showers were put on for me, but I wasn't happy at all. But now I treasure all my babies. I got new tattoos of most of them, they're my reminders.

You see when you don't have power, and you get it, it feels good. It feels like nobody could touch you. It feels like, I don't know how to explain it, it just feels really good to finally be in power and walk down the street knowing that nobody's going to walk in your way. Or when you're walking down the sidewalk and they see you coming, they're going to look at you, and they're going to get out of the way.

When you have control, and when you know you have control, everybody around sees it. If I walk into a house and I see some girl, who is fronting, I think you're a bitch already. I say that because I stepped into this hood house, and I'm in a bad space, but I don't care. I'm watching, but the people think I'm innocent, and this girl is trying to act like she was all gangster. She had baggy clothes, and she was really trying to talk like deadly TV slang. I looked at her, and she wouldn't come around me.

I knew why she wouldn't because she was a fake-ass bitch. I would use her and others like her for everything just 'cause how they present themselves. They're out there too much. You read everything like their body language, and you see them make themselves vulnerable to people when they walk in. When they're in the hood, it makes them look stupid, man; it makes them look real stupid.

People do this stuff to get their dope. The street life is all about addiction. Drinking, money, pot, respect, you want to get that high life you never had in your childhood. It's like you're always starving. Then you get it, and you splurge on it. Then you are back in debt again, you have to go and work it off, over and over and over again. Some people just can't make it out; they are just wicked addicted. Some are so addicted to the drug, to the dope that they are selling, some of them die, but some of them make it out.

But you see it's tough. Because when you feel hopeless and you are so caught in your cycle it's tough. Think about it, you're up here and you know that you paid your dues through your blood. You could say that you bleed in bleed out. Then now you're slowly going back down, but you still have that reputation. But now you're a junkie, and you feel hopeless. You can't even judge that; you know someone is at their bottom.

A year and a half ago, a year ago, I didn't, I say, two years ago, two and a half years ago, that's when the difference became real for me. That's when I lost my dad and I had nothing to live for. Well, I wasn't living for my dad; it's just hard losing a parent. It's hard losing a parent that you love so much. After that, I didn't even care. I didn't have any hope if that answers it. It was hard burying a parent. It added on, and it got too deep for me...It was hard.

I hate this feeling, you know?

I started dealing with my addictions. Well, you live by the sword, you die by the sword. I will give you an example. Someone that I trusted found out that I was cut up and him reaching out sparked that little bit of hope that I had. So I come here, and I want help, but I don't know what I need because I have never gone this far. He tells me to go to detox. Okay go to detox, and I accomplished that. What's next? Time to go to treatment. I go to treatment and complete that because I am at my rock bottom. He helps to find stable housing, and I want my kids back. So I get put in a shelter for a bit.

I have my two oldest kids, get a place, then I start counselling. I have been going to a counsellor for about a year and a half now. I have started talking about my hurts and the fucking pain. Even though I would heal a bit in the past, I would fall off and drink, but I quit using dope.

Before when stuff would come up, it would get so intense that I wouldn't know what to do with myself. I didn't know the tools to use. So I kept on slipping and slipping, but I wouldn't stay there. I wouldn't get deep like I use to. I would just get back up and start using what was given to me. Like with the STR8 UP program, I started to see myself as a person of value because they said I was valued. So I started working towards goals that I had.

It's like so many little steps that you got to take. There's a lot of barriers, and everything that you got to go through initially if you want to live, you want to break the cycle, and you don't want to see your little ones doing that, then you will do anything that it takes, no matter what. But if you just have one foot in and one foot out in the other world, it's not going to work. Your fucking world is going to crash on you anyways, so don't even try. You know I can play this part where I'm perfect, I'm good, nothing's going wrong with me. Then go out there and drink, try to be gangster and shit like that. And you know, I'm good, but that's not going to work, your whole world will crash on you. You need to be balanced—emotionally, physically, mentally, and spiritually.

i know i jus woke up ..lol but ya me n my homies
...NATIVE SYNDICATE....

Jorgina

I was born in Edmonton and my mom was very young when she had me. I don't know how old she was when she had me, but she had me and my brother between the ages of fifteen and eighteen. My brother is fourteen months older than I, and my mom and my dad were in their addiction, alcoholism, and they didn't have any kind of stability. So the story that my dad told me when I met him years later was that they were moving, changing homes, and they didn't want us in the way and they couldn't properly care for us. So they put us in a taxi cab and sent us to a relative's house. Social services were called as nobody was at the home and so we were apprehended. There is no record of whether my parents made an effort to try and get us back, but I did find out later on that my mom never put me down. I also was told that she, when I was in her care, that she dressed me as, like, I guess, a little gangster, like she put me in jean jackets, and jeans, and she had little bandanas around my head and little track, baby tracksuits and what not. But she did instill that love or connection to me when I was young.

So I already know I had an established sense of love, that was, and I remember that feeling of trying to look for that afterwards and I was surprised when I didn't get it from the adults around me. I just wanted people, somebody, to love me. So I really clung to my older brother early in my life. I remember that he was the constant in my life and I am really grateful for that because I can't imagine what would have happened if he wasn't there.

Early on in my life I remember lots of different people coming and going in my life. These were the different foster parents and families that I was sent to go and live with. I remember lots of strange men. I remember sexual molestation. I am guessing I was maybe two and before that there is one memory of me being in a crib and a man inside my diaper. So I would say maybe eighteen months, two years, I know I wasn't walking yet. I also remember being lifted out of my crib by my brother as a foster house that we were in was on fire. I remember being handed to a fireman through the window and him carrying me down the ladder, and putting me in the

back of a cop car, and that was our last day at that foster home.

Once we were apprehended, it was really about my brother and I sort of facing the world together. That's what it felt like, me and my brother against the world. I wouldn't listen to the foster parents, only to my brother as he was my constant. I know my brother didn't talk a whole lot and he was very quiet, so we had this bond that was almost like we communicated without talking. I don't know if that is just something that kids do, but that's what we did. I emulated everything that he did. I wanted to be like him. We took this trip with our social worker to Fort McMurray and we were in a home that was considering adopting two First Nations children and they were East Indian. I remember the guy watching my brother and I, and we met eyes and then he looked at the social worker, and he shook his head no. So when we were taken away, it was almost by that point, I was already thinking nobody wants me. Nobody wants us and so there was no sense of stability. There was no my own room, with my own bed, and no constant figures in my life except the social worker and my brother. That was my perspective. I don't remember times of playing, I don't remember laughing a whole lot, if anything. I remember crying and not understanding why I was crying, and there was no memory of my mom at that point, like I just had no memory of my mother, nothing.

The last foster home we were in was a family just outside of Edmonton, and I remember the white house, your typical farmhouse. I was four and I remember the foster dad Gary. He had a head full of red hair, and it felt like he didn't want me around. I remember a few times wanting to hug him and sit on his lap, and he always shooed me away. He never was violent or physically abusive or anything but I always felt like I was in his way. So I just learned to not talk to him. I learned to not approach him if I needed something. I remember like the other foster kids and their kids tickled me literally till I thought I was going to die. I couldn't breathe. I went into an anxiety attack and passed out. I remember coming to and the sun was shining and we were on the trampoline, except there was no body there, they literally tickled me until I passed out. So I remember feeling traumatized. I can't believe this happened to me and I couldn't make sense of it and I remember trying to tell the foster mom and crying and her turning it around like it was my fault, like, that's how I felt. I did something wrong and I know that there was, by that point, there was sexual abuse happening by

my two brothers, my older two foster brothers.

They were more like little sexual games, like kissing games, and I was like somebody's wife, it was just really, I couldn't understand it, but I went along with it because again I was looking to fit in, and because I was outnumbered. I also started to see that. I wanted to play in the dirt, I wanted to play with trucks and Lego because that was the only way that I could fit in and play with. There was no other girls, there was no other little girls to play around with and I didn't get to wear dresses and stuff a lot.

I remember wearing cords and jeans and just really being a tomboy, and my hair was long and I remember I had these long bangs that kept getting in my eyes, and they were always in the way, and the foster mom never cut them, and I don't know why. The other memory that I have from there was the oldest brother had like a dirt bike, and I just thought it was the coolest thing, and I begged him to take me on it. So one day when the foster parents weren't home, he took, he put me on the back of the bike and we went down the lane to the main road and he turned around and came back, there's that coil on the back of the bike, and its hot so my leg actually got burnt to that, so the, when I got off the bike it tore my pants, and I had this huge burn on my lower right shin, and I didn't want to get him in trouble. So somehow I already figured out how to, about what got people in trouble and what didn't and so I remember going to change my pants and we tried to keep it a secret. I don't know how long the secret lasted for, all I know is I was taken to the hospital later because I had this huge blister on my shin that I tried to keep from my foster mom finding out. I remember the day that he got found out, and he got his bike taken away and how much he looked at me and hated me, he resented me, and he wasn't my friend after that, and it was shortly after that we were adopted.

I remember being downtown Edmonton, and I remember looking up at the building and how tall it was, and I remember the elevator ride and how my stomach felt, the doors open and we went down this long hallway and into this room, and I saw my adopted parents for the first time. My mom to be, I thought she was really beautiful. She was wearing this big white sweater and jeans, and she came down to my level and opened her arms. So I went and gave her a hug. My adoptive dad had this huge beard and he was really intimidating looking to me. But he picked me up and he carried in his arms and we went down the elevator ride.

I remember one of my first school experiences as being absolutely traumatizing. It was at a Halloween dance where everybody was dressed up in their costumes, there were strobe lights, and I was terrified. I didn't know where to be. I had no friends and I didn't know where my brother was, so I stood in the hallway crying. Someone found my brother and they sent us home. It was after this that we moved because our parents didn't think that this place would be very good for us. When we moved I was six years old and in grade one. My parents put me in skiing at this time and I remember they made me go without poles so I would learn my balance, and they would really push me to do things their way. One time, I wouldn't get up, being a kid, and it got my mom really mad and she took it really personally. She would grab my arm and I would just fall back in the snow and it was here that I began to see how abusive my mom could be when she was angry. I wasn't trying to provoke her, but at that point that is how I related to adults, especially adults in my life, because I had no mentoring, guidance, or love. My dad never got angry. He did abuse me though at the house when my mom wasn't around. I remember it happening more often after my parents adopted my brother and sister.

I started to see my parents had lots of rules but they were more on how we behaved in public. We all had to sit quietly and could only speak when spoken to. Lots of pressure to be on our best behaviour when we were in public. So being ourselves was never encouraged and my mom always dressed us up really nice if we went out and because of the skewed relationship with my dad and the abuse was happening probably five or six times a week. I found out it was happening to my sister and we never talked about it. It was something we knew was happening and that was like our bond, weirdly enough, it was like, that's what we based our relationship on.

My mom would become somebody different when everybody was around. She was outgoing, she was fun, she was nice to me. I would say, can I go to so and so place and have a sleepover? and I knew that because she had a friend there she would say yes. I started to see how I could manipulate the situation to serve me, so whether I would either lie about situations. I had all this stuff I was carrying, so I barely passed grade three. I was troublesome in school. I didn't want to do the school work and I didn't pay attention. I always wanted to goof off and I would back talk to the teachers, so the teachers knew that something was going on.

But it was also at school that I discovered I liked to sing. We would the song "Country Roads" and a lot of other folk songs. We would sit in a circle in the gym and I just loved it. I remember just that I wanted to learn all these songs and sing the loudest. So going to school finding music helped me get out of my shell. After school one day, I came home and there was a piano in our living room. It was beautiful. It had a mirror on top of it and it had, like, this velvet seat and we all went over there and we were banging on it.

I wanted to do well for my parents, for my parents' sake, but I didn't have it in me. I just didn't have the self-worth, self-esteem, or self-confidence because of all the messages I was getting from everybody were so skewed. So I had no self-esteem even though I could do all these things. I would do things but it was on my terms, sort of like a ransom. I'm going to do this and I was making deals. If I do this for my mom, then I can stay over at someone's house. I am going to get my allowance and then with my dad it was okay because he is sexually abusing me and these things are happening right. By that point, around eleven or twelve, my dad became very violent and abusive. One memory I have is he hit me with one of those big rotary old phones. I remember we got spanked, they never used objects to hit us, except the phone that one day, but lots of fists, lots of slaps, lots of backhands as forms of punishment.

Thinking back to school again, it was in grade four or five when I really began to notice racism at school. In grade six I had my first confrontation, not with teachers but with students. Lots of bullying. I was a year younger than everybody and my mom was still sewing my clothes and by this point the other young girls are already getting into makeup, people are talking boyfriend/girlfriends. And here I was overweight, First Nations, with my mom's funky style going to school. Yes, I could play piano, which was my safest time where I felt free from everybody.

I learned in school that I was different. That First Nations people were different. It was at that point too that people would look at me differently. If the "class clowns" made jokes everybody laughed, which was probably their fear of wanting to fit in. With everything being said at school and the abuse at home, I felt unattractive. I didn't think that I was pretty. I didn't feel like a girl and got along better with boys. Girls, when I was growing up, were supposed to be this white girl who always had nice new modern clothes, brand names and were allowed to wear makeup and perfume. They were supposed to be flirty, popular, and athletic.

One day a guy at school was saying that Indians were drunks who sat on the bench outside the Canmore Hotel. Another guy saying that all Indians are drunk. When these were said everybody looked at me but nobody said anything. I just didn't know how to stand up for myself at this time, I didn't have it in me. After that I started hearing the words *squaw*, *wagon burner*, *dirty Indian*, and people would say these things to each other. I don't think they were thinking about me, but they would say it and then everybody would realize that I was in the room. It became this unspoken sort of thing that happened. To the point that one time I crashed somebody's sleepover because I didn't get invited. I rode my bike over there and she was having a party and I went in and started crying because I couldn't believe she didn't invite me. All of our friends were there and her dad had to kick me out of her house because I wouldn't leave. I felt totally betrayed. It was at that point when I started to become angry and I started to talk back. My intention now was to hurt other people with my words.

It was in grade nine that I began to physically fight back. This kid, this little fucking bastard goes, "Hey squaw!" I felt like I was kicked in the stomach and my face got all red. He goes, "Hey squaw, do you speak English?" and he said it with a Native accent. I turned around and I said, "Get up," and there was, like, fifteen kids just standing around at lunchtime and I kicked him in the side of his leg, hard. I told him to get up, so he stands up and he goes, "What are you going to do?" I grabbed him by the hair, literally, and I pulled him outside, and I didn't let go of his hair. I was so mad I bashed his head into the door. I pulled him outside and he's trying to say that he was just kidding. I was pushing him and I remember I was trying to hit him. Just how could you fucking say this? I remember he tried to leave and I grabbed him again, and threw him against the school made of bricks.

Grade ten actually changed me because of all the fighting I did to stand up for myself, but was also holding teachers accountable. That is when Oka happened and there was a shift happening. I stopped skiing and taking piano lessons. I also began to shift my friends and boys were interested in me. I still wasn't allowed to wear makeup but I did. I also talked to my mom and told her I didn't like the clothes she made me, which actually opened up our relationship, because it was at that time that I almost felt like disclosing to her about my dad.

I learned at this time that I could literally be anybody. I could be anybody someone wanted me to be, without selling myself. I could adapt to any situation as I had no fear about walking down a hallway by myself. Because of my music I had some self-confidence at this point, some unrealized self-confidence, and my leadership skills came out too. I had no problem speaking up or speaking out and my writing really helped me to get stuff out. My English teacher I think knew about all the stress I was under and trauma that I had gone through because I actually wrote a paper about it, but I didn't realize I actually wrote it. It was a class writing assignment so I wrote about being lonely. He contacted the guidance counsellor and we had a meeting with the principal and asked if I had to call my parents in because they thought I was borderline suicidal.

He actually gave me a really high mark on the paper as he was somebody I felt safe enough to disclose this to and I wanted to do well in his class because I trusted him, because he believed in me. He told me that I was a fantastic writer and tried to help me do better. And it was here that my grades went from barely passing to near the top of my class. I think he talked to the other teachers as they began to come and talk to me. Plus, I think that they saw in the paper that we went to the media about all the racism that was happening in the school, but the teachers said they didn't know. They knew, they just didn't want to admit it.

Before I finished high school, I began to run away to Kelowna every weekend. I started meeting older men, like in their twentieth and thirties. I lost my virginity and I was hanging out with this one guy. He had his own apartment in Kelowna that I could go sleep there, and we would drink and smoke pot.

They used me basically for sex and then I became more of a pain because they had to feed me. They were older than me and they worked and would party. At one of those parties, I got assaulted but I didn't tell my auntie, who lived in Kelowna, about it. I told her I didn't have anywhere to stay and I was trying to find a place to live. I was basically walking the streets, not street walking, just walking because I had nowhere to go.

I had changed because I become angry again, not angry again, I was angry now. I moved my anger now from hurting others to also hurting myself. Where I wanted to be angry and hurt anyone, even myself. I was drinking. I was getting high. I was resentful and started to have this attitude that if you get in my face, I'm going to fucking show you what I am made of.

I moved to Calgary to be closer to my brother and it was there where I started to watch people and how they responded to me. So some people would call it manipulation, but for me it was codependent. I moved there to flee a situation, and when I got there I remember sitting my brother down and he had his boyfriend there. His boyfriend said I could stay for a week and that's it. I thought my brother would stand up for me and say, fuck that, she's staying with us because I loved him and admired him so much. He didn't stand up for me, and I remember looking at him like and so I felt deceived. I ended up going into a group home, with all seventeen-year-olds from broken homes. It was here where I began to watch people more closely. I started watching people and I stopped talking and I stopped talking and I started actually watching how people related to each other. I observed.

When I turned eighteen, I got a cheque from my reserve for about eighteen thousand dollars, and I met this guy who worked at a gas station. We ended up getting a room from a friend of his, and it was pot smoking every day. I went to the mall and I spent like a thousand dollars just buying clothes. The next day Rob says we should get some coke. Right away I got that feeling in my stomach, that scared feeling because, by then, we only smoked pot and drank. I said to him that I never tried coke, but he told me it was okay and that it was good. I gave him the money and he went and picked up some coke. We went back to the room and we had to stop and buy baking soda, we had a spoon in there. He made the stuff and I watched him load his pipe can, and he did his hit, and he said "Okay, it's your turn." I said "Okay, I don't want very much."

I did it, and I remember how it made me feel, and I felt...It's hard to put into words. It was...I liked the taste. I liked the numbness in my mouth, and I remember thinking, this is a nice euphoric feeling. The thing with coke, when you do it once, you want to keep doing it.

Over the next year and a half, we moved to Calgary and I tried to hold down some work. I started to go out more and wear high heels, long pants that flared out, and lots of makeup. I was really striving to be feminine because I hadn't had any experience doing that. So I would go to the bar and wear short skirts and I was good at pool, and I learned how hustle.

One day, after I got fired from a job, a girl I met asked what I did for money. I told her that my man was working and she asked if I had ever "worked." She asked me, "Have you ever given blow jobs for money?" I'm like no and she looks at me and she goes, "I do and it's very lucrative." I left her and the conversation, but it stuck with me.

I called her the next day and asked her to take me sometime when she went to "work." We went out that day. She told me to make sure that I had makeup on and to not wear a skirt or anything because it was winter. She told me to not look like I was doing it, just try and look normal, to look innocent. She trained me how to do engage with cars. Eye contact and then when you get in ask them if they're a cop. Make them touch you. Then you ask them what they want. I remember how scared I was. The first guy that picked me up was this old guy who had huge thick glasses, and he grabbed me. I said okay can you put your hand down my shirt. I was terrified and scared. He put his hand down my shirt so I said okay you're not a cop, and then I was sitting there and my friend was there watching. Then he grabbed me and he was trying to hug. I got all freaked out and my friend went to the back of the car to write down his licence plate. He drove away for about ten blocks and we went into his apartment and did the deed. He gave me a hundred dollars and we used a condom. He dropped me back off and my friend was still standing there. She asked how much I got and then gave me a high five.

I ended up leaving the guy I was with for another guy who taught me how to boost. He partied hard and I started to do more and more coke. We boosted so much that he soon went to jail and I was by myself again. But I soon met a guy who was being recruited by a gang in Calgary. There was a crew of us that hung out, all First Nations, except for one white guy, Jay. One day Jay asked if I wanted to be his girl because there was a crew that he was trying to be down with but he needed a woman in order to be solid.

At this time, I didn't have an understanding of what the gang was. I knew it had something to do with colours, but I had no conception of what it meant. I knew that when they ran in their crews I was intimidated. I knew they were people not to be messed with, that was sort of my perception. I watched them punch out people but they would be nice to the women because they were the customers. Yet at the same time they didn't hesitate to punch out a woman if she owed. It was absolutely terrifying for me to see that.

The next day we went to a bar and walked downstairs. There were all these guys sitting on one side of the wall they all had their black and white rags on. I was fucking scared. They gave us a bunch of dope and we had an hour to get rid of all of all of it or Jay was going to get a minute. So we went and hustled all the dope. We went back and did the same thing and operated like that for about a month. I got to know all the full patched members and I saw some violence. I saw guys get punched out. I saw guys get stabbed. I saw women get sexually assaulted, but not the women who were in the gang. Women outside of the gang. We would go to the Sisal or some city bar and the guys who didn't have woman would pick up, some girl, feed her with beer and then they would all have their way with her. At the time it didn't look or feel like it was gang rape or anything like that but it was. They had these specific kind of women that they would go after.

The woman that were in the gang were respected. The wives didn't get hit on by the other men. We didn't have to worry about getting raped or assaulted, you don't cross that line. You didn't cross that line. As the wife or as the partner, the girlfriend, I could do pick-ups from the full patches. In a sense I was a mule or a transporter as I was trusted. There's an automatic trust that you're given, if the man's okay the woman's okay, so I was trusted to do those pick-ups.

I wasn't with my guy for very long. There was a fellow that was full patch and he sort of had his sights set on me since the day I joined. The way that he looked at me I knew he was attracted to me. He never said anything and of course he wouldn't because he didn't want to disrespect my guy. Well, my guy ended up pulling a home invasion and getting three years, so I was floating now and this guy wasn't with anyone at the time. One night we were at one of the bro's house in the south and the full patch corned me against a wall, and he said Jay's gone and you're mine. I said okay, partly out of fear, but also because I knew what it would mean for me. I would have protection, he always had dope, I knew he would look after me because he was strong, he had a nice body, and other woman and men respected him.

The female role at the time wasn't to engage in the violence, or the jacking of people. We weren't delegated or nominated to carry out missions. We were there to support. Hold the dope. Clean the house and to provide. If the guys needed "runners," we would go get the smokes and make sure they had booze. To make them happy. And at the same time, they would look after us.

You see, all the couples would run together. We would all hang out together, we would get hotel rooms together. We were like a family and I found my voice in the family. We really tried to honour our role as what a faithful woman looks like and we did. I didn't sleep with other men. It was mostly out of fear, but also because I liked what I had. I liked the power that I had. I could call other guys out on their stuff. If I had to collect, I would. I was given a responsibility and we had mutual power by that point.

When I got pregnant, everybody always bought me milk and food to eat. It was always this unwritten, unspoken thing. They were getting me what I needed, prenatal vitamins, a ham sandwich, a litre of milk. They were respectful that way. They would call and ask if I needed anything. My man had people go out on a mission to go get vitamins and anything else that I needed. He would pay them with pot. I went to the doctor's office twice, no it was more than that, I went like three times because I got an ultrasound twice, and it was important even though our life was chaotic.

I ended up losing all my children to family services, and after that I moved out of Calgary for a while to try and straighten up. I was gone for almost a year and when I returned things changed. The people I knew weren't at the same places. They moved to another part of Calgary. I went there and it was like a reunion to be around everyone again...but it was different too. There were more new faces and because we were dealing in cocaine, there was, it was like we were a family but we didn't recruit people and we didn't have colours. We just, we all sort of, ran together.

Over time the drug trade became more violent. With more money came more guns, automatic weapons on the streets and more violence. I got caught in a lot of scary places with all of this. Lots of people continued to carry brass knuckles and when somebody got a beating, they didn't do it on the street or in the open. It was a different level of violence because you're dealing in more numbers. So people owe more money and then people come down harder. I remember the wars on the street where people who owed money got killed. Somebody would walk up and stick a knife into somebody's back and run, and that person may be found dead, nobody would know. But you would know they had a price on their head because they owed like a hundred dollars. That part was always scary.

I remember before I was in the gang about being on my own and there was this lack of trust in myself because I didn't have confidence. Joining the gang offered me that structure again; I had

something to strive for at the end of every day, even if it was on a daily basis. What we were working towards was good enough for me, and the front or the mask that I was able to put on, because I learned that mask quite young, I'm talking maybe three or four years old I had a mask already, of a how, not letting people in or kicking people out, which-ever. The mask was doing that day, right? It was almost in the gang like that mask saved my life more than once espe-cially from either the violence of the other members or the violence from the people that we were retaliating. There were a few times when I was down and I was thinking, this is what a family really looks like. When I talk about the safety I had with my sisters in the gang, that I haven't experienced that sort of loyalty to one another that I was prepared to give it because I tried to give it to my family and it never had a payback.

There was never honour for it, there was never, man, you have been an excel-lent daughter, thanks for keeping our secrets. There was never any kind of affirmation that, that I was loved, or as a daughter that I was appreciated. So being in the gang, I was told every day that I was solid, awesome, all because I was brother man's wife...

I'm not sure if that was imaginary or if it was real, but I know it was real to me. I valued the power of the gang I had and the guys I looked up to, my bros, that they were respected by even people who didn't know who we were. It was almost like because we were down there, almost as constant figures, we had the power. It was all about drugs, it was never about we're a gang and let's all go hang out. It was about drugs, who was selling the drugs, and so there were other people who could maintain, not their addiction, they maintained the business.

Over time though, I began to feel shame. All this shame and feelings came that I didn't want to deal with, I couldn't. I didn't know how to manage the anger and the shame. I just felt it come up like in my stomach, and I remember swallowing really hard and going okay just stop, right? I was totally outside of my body. I was not present and I thought the only thing that is going to keep me present from going crazy is getting high again, just go drink. I remember I even bought myself a mickey and I was sitting by the river just drinking. I didn't care about getting caught. I was smoking dope, I didn't care. I just didn't care. I had no regard for getting caught, for getting busted, nothing. One night I ended up selling to a cop downtown. So they busted me and I got six months. I did that basically standing on my head.

I went to school, I went to gym, I went to church, I went to AA meetings, it was just trying to do my time, was the way that I looked at it. I had seniority again because of my status on the street.

I got out, and I did the exact same thing three weeks later and sold to another cop. I got two years and was shipped to Edmonton and it was a totally different environment. Same-sex obviously relationships, and it was endorsed and supported and everything that was fine. I put in a request because somebody told me about the healing lodge. It could only house, like, thirty women, and it had a long waiting list but I applied anyways.

I wrote a letter to the warden about why I wanted to go there. I talked about my First Nation culture and that I was looking for something, this is who I am, can you help me? They called me to the bubble the next day and they said you're going to Saskatchewan tomorrow. I was like what? I was only in Edmonton for a week. It was just bizarre to me. That was when I started to see that there might be a higher force that worked in my life.

So I ended up going to Okimaw Ohci Healing Lodge, Maple Creek, Saskatchewan.

In the lodge I began to understand my culture. At first, I didn't understand that when you have a question you give tobacco. So I remember I asked this Elder, I don't understand what you mean by that, and she said, well, if you want to know, I'll take some tobacco, and I'll gladly tell you. I was like, why do you need tobacco?, and how that teaching introduced me to other teachings. When I learned about the scarcity of balance, right, and looking back now at this picture and my understanding now, when I go into the night, that there is, almost like a friend there, all the time, watching out, walking with me, everywhere I went, everywhere I went, driving everywhere I went, and that it never abandoned me or didn't go out of place one night or fall from the sky like all those times I thought. It was this constant motion, just like the sun. I also had no control over it, like the sun coming up every morning. I was trying to control all these things in my life. How people reacted to and their perceptions of me. I had no control over my addiction. I tried to say that I did, but I could not control how much I got, how much I used. If I was working the street, I controlled how many times went out the night, because sometimes I just had enough, and there were times when I would go all night, the next morning, all night again. When I was ragged and raw, and you know, the moon and the sun are things we have no control over. That was

the first part of what I learned about. It was explained to me by an Elder at the lodge, that we don't have any control of what the moon does. Moon will walk with you and she is with you always. So when I learned that I remember it hit me. I had this protection all along. It was overwhelming and how I broke down, and how I understood from that day on, not necessarily there being a respect, but a respect for the teaching, respect for the knowledge and how it brought me closer to my First Nations heritage that I had been disconnected from.

One of the things that, that I discovered about myself and people who have walked this life of addiction, crime, and self-destruction, I really fell into this trap of, and I call it a trap because once you're in it doesn't feel like you can get out of it. I always tried, trying to get something for nothing, the hustle, the gang, what can you. You know, when I was in the life, it was drugs and money, always was my intentions. When I started to recover it was about food and cigarettes, and those things were vital. When I was in my addiction, the drugs and the alcohol took precedent, drugs and the money. So when I speak about making payments on my piano, and having bought it for myself, there was nothing attached to it, and I didn't have to scab anybody to get it, and all the money that I made, you know, by the little contract work, jobs that I had at the beginning of my recovery and then that led into full-time work. I made sure that I had money set aside every month, and so in that it was a new sense of responsibility. The sense of feeling accomplished. Having been able to make payments and the idea working for belongings furniture, clothing, car, gas, insurance, all the things we'll say the "normal" people strive for. Just thinking of maintaining it. It took me a long time to learn that because when you're in the gang, you're just trying to get something for nothing all the time. That was a lot of it and I got really tired of it. I got tired of living like that and even today when I see other people who live in that sort of existence, it kind of bugs me. You just hope that they will one day get it, that understanding that if you want stuff, you got to work for it and you can't steal it.

Looking back, I have learnt that the gang life is all about the hustle. Always. Once you embrace these values, it becomes dishonest. My whole life was based around a mask. When I was wearing it, I didn't feel like I was surviving. It was what I had learnt, what I had come to know. It was what I knew how to act to get what I needed. When I started to need different things, my way to get them had to change too.

So when I needed food and I needed help, I needed to get honest. I couldn't do those things when lying or hustling people. So it changes.

For me the change was drastic. It was overnight. It was overwhelming. I didn't know how to do it so I became depressed and frustrated. Lots of frustration. I, that, I couldn't effing do this. It would have been easier to go back to the manipulation and the hustle. But I couldn't live with myself if I went back.

Having come from where I've come from, this has been my journey. When I started my journey to recovery I didn't have good thoughts about myself. Lots of people told me that I was beautiful or that I was pretty, but I had no belief in it. I always thought they were looking for something. Even when it was from my family, I would shy away, giggle, laugh, or brush it off. I couldn't accept the compliment. But to be able to say it, to myself, and to know it, is huge, absolutely, that's huge, to know my worth.

Meeting my children and rebuilding relationships with them today continues to be the most important, meaningful... magical experience I could ever hope to have.

I continue to remind myself of the quote by Vivian Greene: "Life is not about waiting for the storm to pass... but learning to dance in the rain."

Photograph Captions

page ɪɪ Photograph taken by Faith. The police tape laid over top of the burnt house and angel was meant to symbolize the violence within their lives, but also the innocence that is lost with the burnt Christmas angel ornament.

page ᴠɪ Photograph taken by Faith. This photo was taken to show how First Nations girls are seen on the street, ignored, and walked around. She took the photograph right after the women in the hoop walked by who shifted her purse and took steps away from the girls.

page ᴠɪɪɪ Photograph taken by Chantel. The shoes are symbolic in street spaces and depending on local street codes can be a warning sign or a sign of recognition for someone who has passed away. The colours on the shoes are used to mark territories and explain to others which gang or colours are allowed in the neighbourhood.

page x Photograph taken by Faith. She taught her kids to dial numbers collect on a pay phone if they were ever in trouble. She also explained the importance of phone booths to the street lifestyle, and how they were used to communicate with people across the city, as well as those who were in jail.

page xx Photograph taken by Bev. She took this photograph to explain how she saw herself as the perfect "soccer mom" while in the life. She explained how she would drop her children off at their school and after-school activities while at the same time working for the street gang. The photograph is to represent the dual roles that some street-gang-involved women play, and the importance of playing a role of the good mom for others.

page 15 (left) The arrowhead was found with an ex-boyfriend of mine when we were coming off meth. I found it and it was stained with blood. My ex asked an Elder about the arrowhead and he said that white was a sign of royalty. I never thought myself as royalty at that time, just a kid off the street, so it made me happy to find it. (Amber)

page 15 (right) I took this photo when a brother of mine died. This is to show the face that everything in life is blurry but we need to keep moving forward. We aren't allowed to just sit still in this life. It is always going and that's the hard part. (Amber)

page 16 (left) This is me being pissed off and telling people to fuck off, that I have control of my own life. I am also trying to show that we have to wear a mask in this life. One that tells people I am not to be messed with. (Amber)

page 16 (right) I titled this one "A Good Place for a Picnic." This is the spot that women from the streets are dropped off or disposed of when they are of no use. I went there one day with a higher-up and he told me to go wait by the post as he went back to vehicle. I thought that day I was going to die, but what happened is that he gave me my rag and that's when I became down with the gang. (Amber)

page 17 The black rose holds sentimental value 'cause it holds all of the other colours, and it represents my deceased grandma. The dew drops are to show my soul washing itself, crying away everything. I am trying to wash away my past, but you can't forget about everything if you want to help others. (Amber)

page 18 I had the opportunity to speak at a forum while I was in detox. I read a poem to talk to the people there as I saw women who were trafficked, and I knew how to traffic women. I never sold women, but I did put them on the street. (Amber)

page 19 This is a picture of myself with one of my cats. I have always been drawn to cats and them to me. They help me to relax and understand that there are other things in life besides the hustle. It was through this cat that I started to learn to love again. (Amber)

page 20 This image is to reflect back on everything and remind me that I am alive. Again, I love cats and the image of the cat is to remind me of where I have come from, but unlike the black rose, the white cat within nature reminds me of life, a life I want to continue to live. (Stock photograph selected by Amber.)

page 33 (top left) This photograph represents myself growing up. I was always told that I was not good enough or pretty enough, and I just wanted to hide. Hiding my face in the corner was where I thought I could hide from everyone because I felt I was not seen or wanted. (Bev)

page 33 (top right) This is an old photograph that I have. This was the first photograph taken of our gang. Prior to this photograph, we were a crew and friends working together in the hustle. However, after this, we became a street gang, moving us into a different direction. (Bev)

page 33 (bottom left) This is the first house that I had out of the hood. In this house I was expected to look after it. At the house the same things were happening after we became a gang, parties and whatnot. In the house I was not allowed to open the blinds, and all the walls were painted black, our colours. (Bev)

page 33 (bottom right) This was taken on a graffiti wall in Saskatoon. This was a motto that we had while in the gang: can't be stopped. I see this with street gangs, where the street gangs continue to grow and spread throughout Saskatoon and other communities. The gang that I was a part of started with friends and now it has spread across the province and many other communities, and it will keep growing till we address the issues related to street gang involvement. (Bev)

page 34 (top left) I took this photograph to represent the relationship I had with police officers. It was always a game with them and I knew how to talk, which got me out of a lot of situations. I have respect now for some police officers, those who take time to build relationships, but I still don't trust them, with everything that happened to me because of them, with my one son who died. (Bev)

page 34 (top right) This is a commemoration of my best friend, who died in the life, and my son, who was killed because of the life. I placed my black rag to show the violence that the life brings, and that it is not always those involved who are hurt. My son died because of a police raid and my friend died from a gang fight that he was not supposed to be a

part of. Both of them are still a part of me and I will never forget. (Bev)

page 34 (bottom left) These are the newspaper clippings that I collected on the day that my house was busted and I took the fall for the gang. I received a federal sentence for trafficking. I thought by doing this I would show my loyalty to everyone and that I would be protected. Little did I know that everything would change while I was locked up. (Bev)

page 34 (bottom right) This photograph is to show that even when we are out of jail we are still being watched, with people waiting for us to mess up. Probation and parole officers need to move beyond the files that they get about us and learn to build relationships with us. It makes more sense to begin to work with people where we are at, and understand why we had to make certain decisions than see us as bad people making bad choices. (Bev)

page 35 (left) This is in my house now and something that I look to everyday. I have to remember that every day is a new day and to enjoy it, that I need to focus on the little pieces of the day that make me happy and not search for a great happiness. My family is everything to me today. To make sure that they are happy, healthy, and safe from what I have had to go through. (Bev)

page 35 (right) This photograph is to represent the life that I have now. Whereas my first house was dark with no light, my house now is bright with things growing and thriving. This is the change that has happened to me. Like the flowers that need light to come in, I can now be the light for others in my life. (Bev)

page 49 This is a picture to show the "stroll" where I used to live. The graffiti represents the image of being happy and what we are told we are all supposed to have. The small line of grass is the small space that many of us have to walk, that we are told to see the happiness. But really, the only places that are open is the street. (Chantel)

page 50 This photograph represents what many young girls on the streets are trying to do: they are trying to get out, but they believe a colourful life that is promised to them. However, it is a myth, and something that cannot ever be truly achieved. (Chantel)

page 51 This photograph represents my addiction. It is to represent a lack of hope and despair that addiction brings. For myself, hanging my head shows that I don't know what to do, what is next, and where I go from here. (Chantel)

page 52 This photograph represents that although there is despair in this life, many of us still have love and hope for others. The hands represent all of us in this together and our connections to each other. The hands make me think of the person's hand. What were they thinking? What were they feeling? (Chantel)

page 53 This photograph was taken just outside Okimaw Ohci Healing Lodge. It was here that I began to connect with Indigenous spirituality. This place allowed me to begin to heal and address some of the traumas of my life. (Chantel)

page 54 (left) I took this photograph to represent the shift and importance that First Nation Cree spirituality has had on my life. The importance of spirituality has helped me to learn forgiveness but also how we are all connected. It is because of this that I can continue to work on myself. Even though there may be setbacks, I can always turn to spirituality. (Chantel)

page 54 (right) I took this photograph after a programming exercise. The faces represent all of the different masks that I have had to create and wear while I was in the life. The goal was to take all of the masks and burn them so that there is only one mask left, the mask of who we are today. This exercise helped me to begin to let go. (Chantel)

page 55 I took this photograph because so many people think that the hood is place of death and destruction. This was painted on the road and it reminds me that I am alive. I believe that we all need to realize that it is good to be alive, and that to be alive for me now is to be free of addiction and violence. (Chantel)

page 70 (left) This was taken right outside of my first school. It was here where I was bullied and learned to fight back. By fighting I was able to gain status by showing people I would never back down. (Jazmyne)

page 70 (right) This photograph represents the relationship of First Nations with Canada. The flag being ripped and frayed is to show that this is how First Nations and Indigenous women are treated in Canada. That we are discarded and that Canada is not as innocent as it wants others to believe. (Jazmyne)

page 71 (left) I took this photograph to show the destruction and dirtiness that happens on the reserve. It is not like this everywhere, but where I came from this is what I remember as a kid. That things are never nice and clean. (Jazmyne)

page 71 (right) I took this to show the issues of addictions and what happens with trauma. Like the photograph of the ripped Canadian flag, this is where the trauma began, through colonization, and the needle represents how many of us are trying to cope with that trauma. (Jazmyne)

page 72 (left) This is the tag of the gang that I joined. I would put the tag up in my neighbourhood to let people know who controlled the neighbourhood. The tag and the gang became who I was, I was no longer Jazmyne, and I was ready to do anything for the gang. (Jazmyne)

page 72 (right) I took this photograph to show how individuals are faceless in the gang. That all we are in this life is the colour that we wear. (Jazmyne)

page 73 (left) I took this photograph of my daughter and the tipi to show how I am trying to raise my children today, to be proud of who they are, Saulteaux. It was culture and going back to my reserve to focus on my traditions that has helped me on my healing journey. (Jazmyne)

page 73 (right) This photograph again shows the innocence that I want to give to my children, that I was never given. The horse is important in my culture and it is by providing these experiences that I hope I can steer my children from ever having to go through. I have lived this life so that my children don't have to. (Jazmyne)

page 86 I took this photograph to show the impacts that have happened to Indigenous Peoples because of colonization. My daughter represents young Indigenous women and what has happened. The sign says "save from sin," which represents the residential schools that took our children away from us. The "for sale" sign represents that our children are still being taken away and sold on the streets. Because of this our children lose their innocence way too early in their lives. (Faith)

page 87 This photograph represents how our young girls are continuously taken away by the state and how we are treated. We are treated as faceless and nameless when we go through the social systems that are supposed to be there to help us and protect our children. (Faith)

page 88 (left) I took this to show that when I was in the life, the gang was my life. It was who I was from the time I woke, to the time I went to sleep, if I went to sleep. It was more than a group to me, it was my family and is my family. (Faith)

page 88 (right) This photograph was our motto. Regina is known as sin city. The tag and letters refer to the codes that we lived by on the street. NDJM means, never die just multiply. While TDWR means, till death we ride. This is how we were able to recruit impressionable people. That when you are a part of us, you become something bigger than yourself. For youth and young adults who have very little, this is a way to say that there is more out there, if you are willing to take it. (Faith)

page 89 (left) This photograph is of my first partner. He recently passed away but I have always had a place for him. I am his baby mom, the first to carry his son, who would have been the legacy. All of the brothers and sisters recognized this and no one would try anything on him or me. You see, I am known to be rank on the streets, because I can fight, and we had one another's backs all the time. Even though he was the seen by others as a tough guy, because of our relationship we would tell and show each other a side we were too afraid to show others. As you see, in this picture he cared for his kids very much.

He was more than just a gang member. He was a father. He was a partner. He loved the people around him, like anyone does. This is what people forget, that we are more than just gang members, we are people just looking to survive. (Faith)

page 89 (right) This is the jail mail that I have received over the years from my partners. In these letters they are able to express themselves openly, and when you read them you see a lot of hurt. They pour out a lot of the hurt that they are feeling and can't show when they are locked up because if they do, they will be seen as slipping or being a bitch, putting them at risk of attack from others. (Faith)

page 90 (left) I took this photograph to show the new brotherhood that we are looking to build. This was after one of them died from a drug overdose and all of the members showed up at the funeral. If people from outside saw us, they would see us as a street gang because of the vests and the way we look. However, we are about giving back to the community and giving opportunities for those looking to escape the street gang lifestyle. This is what a true brotherhood is all about. (Faith)

page 90 (right) This is the first picture that I have of my first grandchild. I am so proud of my daughter to be carrying this child, and for myself to be around for it. This was one of the happiest days of my life, knowing that I was going to be a grandma. However, I am also scared because I know what I had to do to protect my daughter and what we lived through, and I hope that she doesn't have to do any of what I had to do. (Faith)

page 91 I took this photograph to show my faith. I did not see Indigenous spirituality as a way to live my life because I have always known myself to be a Christian. When people tell me that I have to follow Indigenous spirituality to heal, I shake my head. We all have our own paths and as long as we work on protecting ourselves and learning to connect to things that are greater than ourselves, we can find peace and healing. (Faith)

page 108 (left) This photograph was taken where I grew up in my adoptive home. It was a beautiful place and breathtaking. Despite the beauty, there was a lot of horror that took place here. I never felt that I belonged and could never do anything right. So what this shows is that even though something may look beautiful, there are always secrets that no one wants to talk about. (Jorgina)

page 108 (right) This photograph was taken right after I lost my children to the state. I am trying to put on a face that tries to show I don't care. But the truth is I was hurting so much inside, but I had to show that I did not have emotions. I am also in the life because of how skinny I am, which is another thing. We are told we are beautiful as women when we are skinny, and being on the street makes us skinny with the dope. After that day, I went deeper and deeper into my addiction and the street lifestyle. (Jorgina)

page 109 (left) I took this picture at night as I would always be looking down when I was working the street, selling or using drugs. I would never walk with my head up as I was always looking for something, money, cigarettes, drugs, anything. By looking down I learnt how to also see everything around me, without showing people that I was watching. The other reason is that you could see people's shoes, which helped me to see who people are because you can tell a lot by people's shoes, if they are a cop or if they are from the streets. (Jorgina)

page 109 (right) I took this photograph of the moon because it was a constant for me when I was walking back alleys. I remember a grandmother teaching of the moon and how she restores balance and makes sure we don't go too far off our paths. I was always in awe of the moon, especially the full moon, and it was near the end of my addictions that I started to look up more from the sidewalks to the moon, to begin to pull my head up instead of down. (Jorgina)

page 110 (left) This is a picture of me while I was in jail. I was content at this time because I had a roof over my head and food. I had a reputation before I was sentenced to prison and it was here where I met up again with those that I met from the street. So it was not a place that was scary; it was a place that I was actually reconnecting with others. (Jorgina)

page 110 (right) I drew this rose when I was in a women's group of battered women. Artwork, like music, is soothing for me. It takes concentration, and at times it is this concentration that helps me to deal with my addictions and trauma when it gets too great. (Jorgina)

page 111 (left) Music, and specifically the piano, has always had a very special place in my heart. It was through music that I could escape my realities when I was younger. Today, it is a way to make a living, and a way to tell my story. I write music now to tell my story to try and help others who may be experiencing similar things that I have gone through. The first legitimate money that I made, I went and purchased a piano that I could have in my home. It gave me so much pride and joy to be able to purchase this and show to myself that I am moving forward. (Jorgina)

page 111 (right) This photograph is the prairies opening up to the mountains, like the earlier photograph of the mountains and the lake. The beauty of the picture symbolizes a peacefulness that I have now found. The openness of the prairies with the mountains reflects how I see the opportunities that I now have, with the mountains reminding me that it will not always be easy, but the journey will be worth it. (Jorgina)

page 112 This photograph reminds me of power, strength, and perseverance. I have come such a long way in my life, from childhood trauma, addictions, street lifestyles, the gang life, sex work, and everything in between. This photograph was taken right after I received the Aboriginal Order of Canada, from the Congress of Aboriginal Peoples. Right after this, I started to work with the Murdered and Missing Indigenous Women and Girls Inquiry, as I am trying to give back to the community and protect other Indigenous women from the life I have had to live. (Jorgina)

Bibliography

Anderson, Elijah. *Code of the Street: Decency, Violence, and the Moral of Life of the Inner City*. New York: W.W. Norton, 1999.

Castleden, Heather, Theresa Garvin, and Huu-ay-aht First Nation. "Modifying Photovoice for Community-Based Participatory Indigenous Research." *Social Science & Medicine* 66, no. 6 (2008): 1393–1405.

Comack, Elizabeth, Lawrence Deane, Larry Morrissette, and Jim Silver. *Indians Wear Red: Colonialism, Resistance, and Aboriginal Street Gangs*. Winnipeg: Fernwood Press, 2013.

Cruikshank, Julie. *Life Lived Like a Story: Life Stories of Three Yukon Native Elders*. Lincoln: University of Nebraska Press, 1992.

Dorries, Heather, Robert Henry, David Hugill, Tyler McCreary, and Julie Tomiak, eds. *Settler City Limits: Indigenous Resurgence and Colonial Violence in the Urban Prairie West*. Winnipeg: University of Manitoba Press, 2019.

Ermine, Willie. "The Ethical Space of Engagement." *Indigenous Law Journal*, no. 6 (2007): 193–203.

Fontaine, Nahanni. "Surviving Colonization: Anishinaabe Ikwe Street Gang Participation." In *Criminalizing Women: Gender and (In)Justice in Neo-Liberal Times*, 2nd ed., edited by Gillian Balfour and Elizabeth Comack, 113–29. Winnipeg: Fernwood Press, 2014.

Freng, Adrienne, Taylor Davis, Kristyn McCord, and Aaron Roussell. "The New American Gang? Gangs in Indian Country." *Journal of Contemporary Criminal Justice* 28, no. 4 (2012): 446–64.

Grekul, Jana, and Patti LaBoucane-Benson. "Aboriginal Gangs and Their (Dis) Placement: Contextualizing Recruitment, Membership, and Status." *Canadian Journal of Criminology and Criminal Justice* 50, no. 1 (2008): 59–82.

Grekul, Jana, and Petrina LaRocque. "'Hope Is Absolute': Gang-Involved Women— Perceptions from the Frontline." *Aboriginal Policy Studies* 1, no. 2 (2011): 132–60.

Grossman, Michele. "Out of the Salon and into the Streets: Contextualizing Australian Indigenous Women's Writing." *Women's Writing* 5, no. 2 (1998): 169–92.

Hall, Ronald E. "Cool Pose, Black Manhood, and Juvenile Delinquency." *Journal of Human Behavior in the Social Environment* 19, no. 5 (2009): 531–39.

Hallsworth, Simon. *The Gang and Beyond: Interpreting Violent Street Worlds*. New York: Palgrave MacMillan, 2013.

Hallsworth, Simon, and Tara Young. "Gang Talk and Gang Talkers: A Critique." *Crime, Media, Culture* 4, no. 2 (2008): 175–95.

Henry, Robert. "'I Claim in the Name of…': Indigenous Street Gangs and Politics of Recognition in Prairie Cities." In *Settler City Limits: Indigenous Resurgence and Colonial Violence in the Urban Prairie West*, edited by Heather Dorries, Robert Henry, David Hugill, Tyler McCreary, and Julie Tomiak, 222–47. Winnipeg: University of Manitoba Press, 2019.

——. "Social Spaces of Maleness: The Role of Street Gangs in Practicing Indigenous Masculinities." In *Indigenous Men and Masculinities: Legacies, Identities, Regeneration*, edited by Kim Anderson and Robert Alexander Innes, 181–96. Winnipeg: University of Manitoba Press, 2015.

——. "Through an Indigenous Lens: Understanding Indigenous Masculinity and Street Gang Involvement." PhD dissertation, University of Saskatchewan, 2015.

Henry, Robert, and Chelsea Gabel. "It's Not Just a Picture When Lives Are at Stake: Ethical Considerations and Photovoice Methods with Indigenous Peoples Engaged in Street Lifestyles." *Journal of Educational Thought/Revue de la pensée educative* 52, no. 3 (2019): 229–60.

Henry, Robert, Caroline Tait, and STR8 UP. "Creating Ethical Research Partnerships: Relational Accountability in Action." *Engaged Scholar Journal* 2, no. 1 (2017): 183–204.

Israel, Barbara A., Amy J. Schulz, Edith A. Parker, Adam B. Becker, Alex J. Allen III, Ricardo Guzman, and Richard Lichenstein. "Critical Issues in Developing and Following CBPR Principles." In *Community-Based Participatory Research for Health: Advancing Social and Health Equities*, 3rd ed., edited by Nina Wallerstein, Bonnie Duran, John G. Oetzel, and Meredith Minkler, 31–46. San Francisco: John Wiley & Sons, 2018.

Kirkness, Verna J., and Ray Barnhardt. "The Four R's—Respect, Relevance, Reciprocity, Responsibility." *Journal of American Indian* Education 30, no. 3 (1991): 1–15.

Kontos, Louis, David Brotherton, and Luis Barrios, eds. *Gangs and Society: Alternative Perspectives*. New York: Columbia University Press, 2005.

Kovach, Margaret. *Indigenous Methodologies: Characteristics, Conversations, and Contexts*. Toronto: University of Toronto Press, 2009.

Louis, Renee Pualani. "'Can You Hear Us Now?' Voices from the Margins: Using

Indigenous Methodologies in Geographic Research." *Geographical Research* 45, no. 2 (2007): 130–39.

Messerschmidt, James W. *Flesh and Blood: Adolescent Gender Diversity and Violence.* Lanham, MD: Rowan and Littlefield, 2004.

Mitchell, Claudia. *Doing Visual Research.* Los Angeles: Sage, 2011.

Richardson, Chris, and Liam Kennedy. "'Gang' as Empty Signifier in Contemporary Canadian Newspapers." *Canadian Journal of Criminology and Criminal Justice* 54, no. 4 (2012): 443–79.

Rios, Victor. *Punished: Policing the Lives of Black and Latino Boys.* New York: NYU Press, 2011.

Scarrow, Kristine. *STR8 UP and Gangs: Untold Stories.* Saskatoon: Hear My Heart Books, 2010.

Totten, Mark. "Preventing Aboriginal Youth Gang Involvement in Canada: A Gendered Approach." *Aboriginal Policy Research Consortium International (APRCi),* no. 55 (2010): 255–79.

Totten, Mark, and Native Women's Association of Canada. "Investigating the Linkages Between FASD, Gangs, Sexual Exploitation and Woman Abuse in the Canadian Aboriginal Population: A Preliminary Study." *First Peoples Childe & Family Review* 5, no. 2 (2010): 9–22.

Tuhiwai-Smith, Linda. *Decolonizing Methodologies: Research and Indigenous Peoples.* 2nd ed. Dunedin: University of Otago Press, 2013.

Vizenor, Gerald. *Surivance: Narratives of Native Presence.* Lincoln: University of Nebraska Press, 2008.

Wang, Caroline C. "Photovoice: A Participatory Action Research Strategy Applied to Women's Health." *Journal of Women's Health* 8, no. 2 (1999): 185–92.

Wang, Caroline, and Mary Ann Burris. "Photovoice: Concept, Methodology, and Use for Participatory Needs Assessment." *Health Education & Behavior* 24, no. 3 (1997): 369–87.

Wheaton-Abraham, Jyl M. "Decolonization and Life History Research: The Life of a Native Woman." *IK: Other Ways of Knowing* (May 2016): 112–21.

Wilson, Shawn. *Research Is Ceremony: Indigenous Research Methods.* Winnipeg: Fernwood Press, 2008.

Other Titles from University of Alberta Press

Keetsahnak / Our Missing and Murdered
Indigenous Sisters

Edited by KIM ANDERSON, MARIA CAMPBELL
& CHRISTI BELCOURT

A powerful collection of voices that speak to
antiviolence work from a cross-generational
Indigenous perspective.

Disinherited Generations

*Our Struggle to Reclaim Treaty Rights for First
Nations Women and their Descendants*

NELLIE CARLSON & KATHLEEN STEINHAUER
with LINDA GOYETTE

Foreword by MARIA CAMPBELL

Two Cree women fought injustices regarding the
rights of Indigenous women and children in Canada.

More information at uap.ualberta.ca

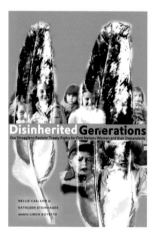